The Family Secret

THE FAMILY SECRET

DOMESTIC VIOLENCE IN AMERICA

WILLIAM STACEY
ANSON SHUPE

BEACON PRESS   BOSTON

Beacon Press books are published under the auspices
of the Unitarian Universalist Association of Congregations in North America,
25 Beacon Street, Boston, Massachusetts 02108
Published simultaneously in Canada by
Fitzhenry & Whiteside Limited, Toronto

Printed in the United States of America

(hardcover) 9 8 7 6 5 4 3 2 1
(paperback) 9 8 7 6 5 4 3 2 1

Stacey, William A.
  The family secret.

  Bibliography: p.
  Includes index.
  1. Family violence—United States. 2. Family
violence—Texas. I. Shupe, Anson D. II. Title.
HQ809.3.U5S77 1983   306.8'7'0973   82-73965
ISBN 0-8070-4144-0
ISBN 0-8070-4145-9 (pbk)

Acknowledgments

A large number of persons working "in the trenches" to do something about family violence have helped sensitize us to the problems which confront any simple remedy. Not all these persons can be named, for in some instances we promised anonymity to protect informants from possible recriminations by their bureaucratic superiors. We are pleased to thank publicly the directors and staffs of the women's shelters where we did much of our research, particularly Gail McIntosh, Christine M. deLange, Donna Pope, and Abbie Troy of the Domestic Violence Intervention Alliance of Dallas, Inc. Both Fran Denis, director of Friends of the Family in Denton, and Gerry Beer in Dallas, Texas, gave us the inside view of the politics (and obstacles) of starting up shelters in different communities. Marilyn Harris, former director of the shelter in Arlington, Texas, was also most helpful and patient in alerting us to the differences in how shelters are created and managed. Our research activities at the state level were invaluably smoothed out for us by Debby Tucker and Eve McArthur (themselves former shelter directors), currently co-directors of the Texas Council on Family Violence, who became strong advocates of this project. Betty Button, Duwain Dumas, and Leslie Lemon of the research staff of Texas state senator Chet Brooks, chairman of the Texas Senate Subcommittee on Human Resources, also assisted our efforts with publicity, contacts, and moral support. We are particularly grateful to Senator Brooks for his encouragement. Ellen Fischer, formerly with the Texas Department of Human Resources and now director of the Austin Center for Battered Women, helped put the bureaucratic realities of monitoring domestic violence into perspective. Allan Dietz, a psychologist employed by the Austin Police Department, and Lonnie Hazelwood, coordinator of Austin's Child and Family Services Diversion Program for batterers, generously directed us to an often neglected aspect of the family violence story: the police relationship to the men who batter women and children. Police officers Russ Shupe, David Sletto, and Jeffrey Thomas were also enormously important to this study for their special contributions on this subject, as were psychologists Toby Meyer and Melissa Eddy and sociologist Joan Weston. Fort Worth attorneys B. C. Cornish and Sister Shawn O'Reilly and Dallas attorney Mary Neal Sisk helped us to understand the legal complexities (and frequent dead ends) facing battered women who turn to the courts for help, as did several private attorneys for whom we served as consultants in domestic violence cases.

Closer to home, our sociology department chairman, Charles E. Ramsey, and the dean of the College of Liberal Arts of the University of Texas at Arlington, Thomas Porter, provided their continuing support for yet another controversial study. Susan Levisay and Nancy Blackmon were indispensable in helping us prepare the final analysis and manuscript copies for the publisher. And Jack Carter, our colleague and graduate assistant, performed yeoman service as he spent many a tedious hour helping us code data.

Finally, there is (as one might expect) a large number of informants, mostly victims of domestic abuse but also including police, batterers, several judges, and journalists, who will remain anonymous. Nevertheless, their contributions are deeply appreciated. We hope this project will someday benefit them all. No individual will directly profit from the sale of this book. Instead, royalties will be donated to The Family Place, the Dallas, Texas, shelter for battered women and their children where we first began our research.

Contents

Prologue

ABBIE M. TROY, PSYCHOLOGIST

On May 19, 1982, I was called to give expert testimony in the murder trial in Dallas, Texas, of Loretta Swanson. Since I spent two and a half years as the Director of Counseling Services at The Family Place in Dallas (a position which enabled me to come in contact with hundreds of battered women) and am currently working toward a Ph.D. in psychology, there was little impediment to my testifying as an expert witness on the issues and dynamics of domestic violence. The defending attorney was certain that a murder charge was ludicrous. He felt it could be shown that on the night of his death, Loretta's husband had blocked the door to prevent her from leaving and had threatened to "stomp her ass." As he approached to hit her with her purse (the contents of which he had strewn about the house in an attempt to destroy her credit cards and her wallet), she picked up a gun from the top of the television set and shot twice. The fatal bullet hit the man's shoulder blade and was deflected into his heart.

I had interviewed this woman on two different occasions while she awaited trial. She was terribly depressed and frightened. Her story was like many others I had heard and continue to hear as I work with battered women. I was convinced of her honesty and felt that she certainly fit the mold of the battered woman so aptly outlined in *The Family Secret*. She was a lovely, strong woman who was a victim of abuse in her own home, who saw her husband as a very powerful figure at some times and a terribly needy child at others. The violence in her home fit the cycle described in this and previous studies about domestic violence. Loretta was also economically dependent upon her husband. After our two sessions, I asked her to call me if she needed to talk. I did not hear from her or see her until six months later—the day I was to testify in her trial.

I felt confident that I could contribute to her defense. Certainly, the citizens of the jury would see her economic and emotional entrapment, acknowledge that the threat of impending violence was real due to her past experiences with her husband, and conclude that self-defense was her only alternative to avoiding an imminent, brutal assault.

The jury listened intently as I spoke—I knew they were hearing me and were genuinely attempting to understand the premises I was introducing. The prosecutor was caustic and I felt he aided rather than challenged my testimony, which was going smoothly. I was able to say most of what I had intended to say. What was disturbing, however, was the face of the woman accused of murder. As Loretta sat in front of me, I hardly recognized her. She was motionless, staring into space, obviously disturbed by what she was hearing yet appearing resigned and unaware. Her attorney had informed me before my testimony that things were not going well; his client had admitted during cross-examination that she had a bad temper, and she had contradicted herself a number of times during her testimony.

Between the time I had seen her and the date of her trial, Loretta had lost her job, had been evicted from her apartment, and was drinking heavily. What struck me as I looked out from the witness stand was that I believed in her innocence more than she did. Although she had shot her husband out of sheer terror and in self-defense, that knowledge was not enough for her to defend herself effectively in a court of law. She missed her husband—it was as if her life had lost its purpose in his absence. What she was feeling and conveying during the trial was a tremendous sense of guilt and sadness over the death of her husband. She was also implying that she had spent years minimizing the level of violence in her marriage. She had become a pro at covering up her bruises with makeup. After rationalizing and denying the violence for so long, she had even begun to doubt the severity of its occurrence. As she herself so poignantly asked in her interview with me, "If it really was as horrible as I'm telling you it was, why did I stay with him?" The jury convicted her of manslaughter.

Loretta had raised the fundamental question surrounding this issue. I am able to answer it with the results of studies such as this one and from my own professional experience. She stays because she has few, if any, resources. She stays because there is little or no help for her legally. And she stays because she's been called a provoker and a masochist by misinformed professionals whose attitudes serve to entrench her further in a dangerous situation. All these aspects are thoroughly and accurately explored in the pages of this study. But for me, a therapist who works with families and a woman involved in a successful relationship with a man, she is saying more.

The women of this study (many of whom I have known and worked with) are representative of all women in our culture. They are not necessarily acquainted with violence in their childhood homes, as the rejection of the "generational transfer hypothesis" for the women in this study clearly reveals. They are often effective homemakers and/or employees, and excellent parents. They are more similar to than different from many of the women who will read this book. And, like many women in our culture today, they do not feel complete or successful without a relationship with a man. Women do not marry with the expectation that they will be abused, but often marry with the expectation that marriage will make them whole, worthy human beings. As the case of Loretta so clearly taught me, it was her self-imposed guilt that said if the relationship failed, it was clearly her fault; and as her behavior after her husband's death and during her trial demonstrated, she thought life wasn't worth living without him and maybe she didn't deserve to defend herself after all. While she was married and taking care of her husband, she was able to demonstrate strength and felt needed. The message is clear: Married is better, no matter what the price.

It is, of course, very disturbing to think that women will submit to being brutalized because they have no concrete, immediate choice when faced with an imminent physical assault. It is even more distressing to think that the pressure women feel to be successful in a marriage may contribute to victimization and lead to denial and minimization of terrifying levels of violence in the home. In reading the findings of this study, I was not surprised to learn that violence has been reported to decrease in the homes of those women who returned to husbands after a stay in a shelter. It appears that what these women needed to discover for themselves, and what they had to convey to their spouses, was simply that they had a safe, supportive, accessible alternative—a shelter in the community. The necessity of having this choice is well documented in *The Family Secret*. The choice, however, should be a woman's own. She must exercise her human and legal right not to be victimized, whether she is in her home and her assailant is her spouse or boyfriend, or whether she is on the street and the assailant is a stranger. The need for the community to provide this choice is clear—the alternative of death and continued violence is far too costly to our society. But the need for men and women who are able to confront their own desires and needs for successful relationships must also be examined and dealt with.

As people today marry in record numbers while our culture continues to exhort women to learn and utilize the best and most manipulative techniques to catch and keep their men, it becomes frighteningly clear that we are still far from perceiving relationships between women and men as a pleasant and rewarding feature of mature adult life. Instead, such relationships are often an obsessional and absolute need. Certainly, as we educate ourselves about domestic violence as an occurrence of social importance, so too must we examine the psychological implications of these attitudes and expectations for men and women in our society. For women like Loretta, it is too late. She chose the only option she felt was available—and the price she and her dead husband paid is far too high.

Introduction

This was a troubling book both to research and to write. Domestic violence is an unpleasant subject, and woman-battering, like child abuse, is one of its most sordid aspects. When we began this study several years ago, we could guess many of its intellectual dimensions. Only later, after we became familiar with literally hundreds of detailed case studies, thousands of other violent incidents, and the views of numerous experts in the field, did we fully appreciate the more visceral, emotional levels of the problem of family violence. To us as sociologists and as persons not totally naive about violence (a former professional boxer and a black belt in both judo and karate, respectively), what we came to discover was shocking in its degree and extent. Family violence frequently takes forms that would disgust and horrify many persons if they were more aware of them. For us neutrality became impossible and objectivity a labor.

As other social scientists have observed, family violence is widespread in American society. It can be likened to a cancer, which is part of an organism but which at the same time fatally corrupts and destroys its host. From all indications, it is a growing threat to the future of our whole society. Moreover, it can even be passed on from parents to children, making some families literally training grounds for future generations of violent adults.

Yet at the same time domestic violence often remains a

"family secret." Many public officials ignore it as trivial. Legislators make it a low-priority item in their budgets. Even many of its victims try to conceal its effects from their relatives, friends, neighbors, and co-workers. Sadly, its youngest victims often have no one to turn to or cannot explain their dilemma. Victims of family violence from incest to beatings may remain silent out of fear, embarrassment, or the belief that there is nothing they can do about it. Commonly circulated myths that violent homes are somehow "sick" or abnormal, or, alternatively, "normal," do little to help bring the problem out into the open. Only recently have communities begun to recognize the problem. The nationwide creation of shelters, originally established for battered women but increasingly seen as havens for victimized children as well, is one such response.

So is research. In the past decade sociologists, psychologists, and social-work professionals have aggressively pursued the factors that lead to family violence. We are now beginning to gain a clearer picture of the problem, and thus finding information that in turn can feed back into the efforts of shelters to deal with the victims of violence. In researching this project we analyzed over a two-year period the single largest collection of domestic violence cases ever assembled, including information about not only the victims (women and children) but also the batterers. Our sources are varied and concern different aspects of the problem, but they converge in an overall picture of family violence more complete than studies based on smaller numbers of cases with only partial perspectives. These sources were:

1. The detailed histories of 542 women (and batterers) who entered one of two shelters for physically abused women (Friends of the Family in Denton, Texas, or Family Place in Dallas) between January 1, 1980, and the end of March, 1982. These histories were collected on standard entry forms when women came to the shelters. The forms are required by the Texas Department of Human Resources for any shelter receiving funds from its office and make up the primary source of data in our study.

2. Exit forms for a majority (262) of the women who entered and left Dallas's Family Place shelter during 1980 through 1982, containing the women's evaluations of their shelter experiences and their plans for the future.
3. Follow-up interviews one to two years later with selected women who had been residents of the shelters, focusing on what directions their lives took after they left.
4. 2096 completed telephone interviews with persons who called Dallas's Family Place between January 1, 1980, and December 31, 1982, to speak to trained "Hotline" crisis counselors.
5. Entry-form information on 67 middle- and upper-class women receiving counseling from Dallas's Family Place's "Help Center," designed to aid women not seeking shelter but who nevertheless have to cope with battering males.
6. 67 cases of clients seeking legal aid for divorce at the West Texas Legal Services office in Fort Worth, all of whom had experienced domestic violence.
7. Interviews with 74 widowed, separated, or divorced women who had sought job training help from a Displaced Homemaker Center in Arlington, Texas, during 1979 and who were contacted two years later about any experiences with domestic violence in their previous marriages.
8. Our own informal discussions and formal interviews with dozens of women outside the shelters we studied, as well as with law enforcement personnel, lawyers, social workers, psychologists, and legislators. In some instances we made first-hand observations to appreciate better the viewpoints of those who deal directly with family violence, as when we sat in on therapy sessions with battering men and interviewed their counselors. In addition, we have drawn upon our experiences as consultants to attorneys defending women victimized by abusive men and a generally unresponsive, unsympathetic legal system.

We have chosen to focus much of our study on information gathered from shelters that service battered women and their children for several reasons. One is that by studying this special group of seriously abused women we see the more severe cases of family violence where everyone would agree there are victims. In some families in the total population violence is sporadic, rare, or not literally life-threatening. Many of these victims may not even define themselves as such. To enter a shelter, however, a woman must agree with the professional staff members that she has experienced significant violence. There can be little doubt in deciding whether or not these women have been abused.

A second reason for using this source is that the public in many states is increasingly being asked to fund such shelters with its tax dollars. Taxpayers deserve honest appraisals of the need for these services, who is being helped by shelters, how they are operated, and what actual good they do.

A third reason is more pragmatic. The "family secret" of domestic violence is still too sensitive a subject for pollsters and survey researchers to be able to approach total strangers, randomly picked or not, and barrage them with questions about the most intimate aspects of their lives. This technique has been used, but it has obvious problems. Thus we can have greater confidence in a known group of victims of family violence who have the least reasons for covering up the secret, even if it means that we cannot generalize from these serious cases to every violent family or abuser.

Much research conducted in the past by psychologists and social workers has been handicapped by having only relatively small groups of persons available to study. The weakness of small samples is not that big ones are necessarily better, but that patterns and relationships among various factors are usually easier to see when large numbers of persons are involved. Many people unfortunately shrink back from statistics like vampires from garlic. We want to reassure such readers with two observations. First, we have deliberately kept our statistics descriptive, placing them in tables made as readable as possible so as not to confuse the average reader. Fortunately the patterns we discovered are almost always very clear. These tables appear at the end of the text in Appendix A, where readers may refer to them for further details about our findings. Second, the numbers tell a story that we have tried to humanize with true anecdotes and case histories. Yet in many ways these figures portray a certain grimness that any individual story cannot. Our findings relate the problems of not only the thousands of women in our study, but millions nationally. No individual story can convey that sort of message.

In this book we examine in particular The Family Place in Dallas, Texas (hereafter referred to simply as Family Place), to show a shelter's operations, problems, and possibilities. Those who are familiar with shelters will soon realize that Family Place is in many ways not typical. It is relatively well funded, runs exemplary therapy programs for both women and children, stays in the forefront of offering innovative family violence services through obtaining grants to fund pilot programs, and harbors none of the frictions between staff and supervisory board that plague so many shelters. In the opinions of many workers in other shelters and local family violence experts, Family Place is one of the top two or three shelters in Texas, if not the best. Thus we selected Family Place not only because we had convenient access to it, but also because it can serve as a benchmark for understanding shelters in the 1980s.

Some readers may also wonder if a study of Texas women, children, and battering men is relevant to other states and regions of the United States. They might ask whether the subcultural and historical background of Texas make family violence there a different matter from such violence in, say, Boston, New York, or San Francisco. At first this might seem a reasonable question, but actually there is little reason to think family violence in Texas is different from that anywhere else. For example, in their national survey of domestic violence, sociologists Murray Straus, Richard Gelles, and Suzanne Steinmetz found no significant differences between the amount of such conflict in southern and western families and in northern and eastern families. One could think the "macho" frontier ethos of Texas males might make violence against women more acceptable, but at the same time we can point to the southern tradition of idealizing women as "ladies" and the "weaker sex," which still lingers in spite of the women's liberation movement. In addition, as a region of the country to which so many Americans have migrated, Texas is probably as good a site as any other to study family violence with an eye to its national implications. The dynamics, the processes, the mechanics of the problem are the same. As one colleague stated, "A lead pipe in the head does the same damage in Dallas as in Detroit." Our discussions with professionals in other parts of the country give us no reason to suspect otherwise.

FORMAT OF THIS BOOK

Each of the following chapters answers some particular question or questions about family violence. Each chapter also has another purpose: either to expose readers to the seriousness and scope of family violence, or to explain options that victims of violence have and to present suggestions for improving these options.

Chapter one outlines the scope of the family violence problem and defines the specific types of abuse that we will consider in succeeding chapters. It examines the history of abuse of women and violence against children as well as what we know of battering men.

Chapters two and three analyze the effects of family violence on women and children, respectively, in order to portray their plights when they escape to shelters.

Chapter four probes the backgrounds of battering men in order to identify who these serious offenders are and to understand how they contribute to the dynamics of family violence.

Chapter five considers the various options of staying or leaving that a woman has, ranging from the extreme of passively accepting the violence to the opposite one of literally killing the batterer.

Chapter six focuses on the women's shelter option, explaining what happens once a woman chooses this course, the sorts of aid she can expect, the type of people she will meet and live with for a time, and what further options the shelter can provide her. In addition, we will look at the shelter experience through the victims' eyes. Finally, we will follow a limited number of women after they left the shelters to see what happened to their lives afterward.

Chapter seven examines the legal aspects of domestic violence and the frequent lack of meaningful police response to it. However, it is not our intention to crucify the police, for they work under their own unique constraints. Moreover, they face a different set of problems than do shelter workers and therapists.

Chapter eight presents an overview of our conclusions about domestic violence plus a realistic assessment of the spread of violence in homes throughout our society in the near future. Rather than treat each element in the violent family situation separately as in previous chapters, here we will put the pieces together and examine the total issue.

WILLIAM A. STACEY
ANSON SHUPE
ARLINGTON, TEXAS

The Family Secret

1

BEYOND THE
BURNING BED

ON MARCH 9, 1977, MICKEY HUGHES BEAT HIS FORMER WIFE, FRANCINE, FOR THE LAST TIME. A PERSISTENT ABUSER OF BOTH HIS WIFE AND FOUR CHILDREN, MICKEY HAD BEEN DIVORCED FROM FRANCINE SOME YEARS EARLIER BUT HAD MOVED BACK IN WITH HER AND THE CHILDREN, EVENTUALLY STAYING AGAINST THEIR WISHES. THAT FINAL NIGHT, INEBRIATED, HE BATTERED HER OVER THE ISSUE OF EATING TV DINNERS. HE GRABBED HER BY THE HAIR; PUNCHED HER IN THE FACE AND HEAD REPEATEDLY, BRUISING HER FACE AND SPLITTING HER LIPS; AND THREW GLASS OBJECTS AT HER. HE TOSSED HER COLLEGE NIGHT-CLASS TEXTBOOKS AND NOTES ABOUT THE HOUSE, FORCING HER TO BURN THEM IN THE BACKYARD TRASH BIN. HE THREATENED TO TAKE A SLEDGE HAMMER TO HER CAR TO PREVENT HER FROM ATTENDING ANY MORE COLLEGE COURSES.

MICKEY WAS A VIOLENT MAN. HE HAD A POLICE RECORD AND A DRINKING PROBLEM. ONCE, ON A BITTER WINTER'S NIGHT, HE FORCED THE PREGNANT FAMILY DOG OUT INTO A FREEZING BACKYARD AS SHE WENT INTO LABOR, DELIBERATELY KILLING BOTH MOTHER AND PUPS. THIS MARCH NIGHT, AS HE CALLED FRANCINE A FUCKING BITCH AND A WHORE IN FRONT OF THEIR CHILDREN, MICKEY HUGHES HURLED THE TV DINNERS ACROSS THE DINING ROOM CARPET AND MADE FRANCINE CLEAN UP THE

MESS. WHEN SHE HAD FINISHED, HE DUMPED THE CONTENTS OF THE GARBAGE CAN BACK ONTO THE FLOOR, THIS TIME SMEARING THE FOOD SCRAPS IN HER HAIR AND FACE AS HE CONTINUED HIS OBSCENITIES. HE ORDERED HER TO CLEAN UP AGAIN. THEN, AFTER BACKING HER INTO A CORNER WITH HIS POUNDING FISTS, HE DEMANDED THAT SAME EVENING THAT SHE HAVE SEX WITH HIM. SHE COMPLIED OUT OF FEAR OF A WORSE BEATING. OVER HALF AN HOUR LATER, AFTER HE FELL SATIATED INTO A DEEP SLEEP, FRANCINE STUMBLED BACK TO THE LIVING ROOM AND HER TERRIFIED, TERRORIZED CHILDREN.

MICKEY HAD BEATEN FRANCINE FOR OVER TWELVE YEARS, BUT THAT NIGHT SHE CAME TO THE SUDDEN REALIZATION THAT SHE COULD NO LONGER ENDURE THIS HELL AND ITS SEEMINGLY ENDLESS VIOLENCE. LATER THAT EVENING, AS HE SLEPT, SHE PACKED HER CHILDREN INTO HER CAR (WHICH MICKEY HAD TRIED TO LOCK INSIDE THE GARAGE). SHE WENT INTO THEIR BEDROOM AND POURED GASOLINE ON THE FLOOR AROUND THE BED, THREW A LIGHTED MATCH INTO THE ROOM, AND THEN SPED AWAY FROM A HOUSE ENGULFED IN FLAMES. A NAKED MICKEY HUGHES WAS LATER FOUND BY FIRE FIGHTERS, DEAD OF SMOKE INHALATION. OVER EIGHT MONTHS AFTERWARD, HAVING WAITED IN A LOCAL JAIL WITHOUT BAIL FOR HER CASE TO COME TO TRIAL, FRANCINE HUGHES FACED THE CHARGE OF FIRST-DEGREE MURDER. IN DRAMATIC COURTROOM PROCEEDINGS SHE EVENTUALLY WAS ACQUITTED OF MURDER BY REASON OF TEMPORARY INSANITY.

BEYOND THE BURNING BED

Francine Hughes's ordeal is a true horror story of family violence, recounted in Faith McNulty's best-seller, *The Burning Bed*.[1] Unfortunately, Francine Hughes's beatings, however spectacular her solution for ending them, were not unusual. As we shall show in the pages to follow—and we are by no means the first—violence in families is rampant in American society.[2] Indeed, there is good reason to think it is on the increase. For example, consider only the problem of woman-battering. FBI statistics estimate that a wife is beaten every 30 seconds in this country (or 2,880 women are beaten every day, or 1,051,200 every year). Sociologist Richard Gelles, a well-known researcher in the field of domestic violence, believes that no fewer than two million women are victims of severe physical abuse each year.[3] He and his colleagues Murray Straus and Suzanne K. Steinmetz conducted the first national study where American families were contacted randomly (rather than through social agencies) and asked about violence among their family members. Between one fourth and one third of the thousands of respondents reported experiencing domestic violence, and the researchers considered that proportion a serious underestimate for the general population.[4]

To put the problem of family violence in clearer perspective: Kentucky's Senator Wendell Anderson stated in the *Congressional Record* on March 16, 1978, the fact that while 39,000 Americans died in the Vietnam conflict between 1967 and 1973, at the same time 17,570 Americans also died literally on the home front, from family violence. *Most of these were women and children.* Indeed, if woman-battering and child abuse were defined as medical diseases, then our nation's public health officials would not hesitate to claim we are currently experiencing an epidemic. To state the situation another way: if assault against another person were perceived as a crime, regardless of whether it occurred inside or outside a marriage or home, then domestic violence involving such assaults would be undoubtedly the single most frequently encountered crime by Americans today. It may be the case that we are now simply becoming more attuned to the problem of family violence, and therefore the statistics only seem alarming due to our increased attention. But, more ominously, it may be that family violence is in fact on the rise in absolute terms, that social strains (in particular the stagnating economy) and a spreading cult of violence are producing a sinister, growing pattern of abuse and death threatening the institution most critical to the survival of our and any society, the family. This is a grim possibility that we will consider again later in this study.

Our goal in this book is to answer two important questions about family violence that we pose in advance for readers:

1. How does violence in the home affect the family?
2. What can be done about it?

We want to answer these questions realistically and practically, not only for women who may be trying to decide if they or their children are victims of abuse, or what they can do about such abuse, but also for their friends, brothers, fathers, clergy, and employers who may want to help them find a way out of their violence crises. To such persons we advise: *If you are not a battered woman, or a woman with a battered child, but know one who is, give her this book.*

To answer the two questions above we focus on violence as it affects only women and children. Thus we will ignore battered men, men who are physically abused by their wives and girlfriends. While such a predicament may seem laughable to many readers, it is not, as the staffs of shelters can attest. In the middle of our own study we personally received calls from such men who had learned of our research (they wanted to give us the "other side of the story") and discovered desperate calls made to women's shelters, such as the one from the six-foot two-inch Texas carpenter whose karate-expert wife had landed him in the hospital for the fourth time. There is no reason to think that men are never the targets of violence from women. Indeed, in their comprehensive survey of American families, sociologists Straus, Gelles, and Steinmetz found just as much violence directed by women at men as vice versa.[5] But as Steinmetz has pointed out, husband-beating and male spouse abuse is still a very camouflaged social problem, in part because battered men are reluctant and embarrassed to come forward to talk about their experiences and in part because researchers have been preoccupied with the greater severity of woman-battering. After all, blow for blow, larger, stronger men will in the long run tend to do greater damage to smaller, weaker women than the reverse.[6] We will not be ignoring men in this study, but they are seen here as the perpetrators, not as the victims, of violence. Abuse of men by women, long an ignored and even taboo subject, needs further study.

DEFINING ABUSE

What do we mean by abuse? How we define violence, or abuse, in this book will not satisfy everyone. Some experts would include all forms of abuse toward women and children, such as verbal unpleasantness and emotional callousness (that is, psychological abuse as well as physical battering), on the grounds that whatever its type, abuse can damage. Indeed, we agree that psychological abuse can sometimes have more long-ranging and serious effects than any physical blows that leave visible scars, particularly on children. Some experts would also include virtually any form of aggressive physical contact or punishment of children, such as spanking, in the category of child abuse.

While we understand these views, there are pragmatic reasons to keep our definition of abuse narrow. One simply has to put first things first, and on the list of priorities the physical safety of women and children must come before concerns for their self-images, feelings of self-esteem, and other psychological states. For that reason we define woman-battering much as many women's shelters have been forced to do in order to cope with the avalanche of women actually fleeing from violent men: as physical harm or the immediate threat of such harm. Much of this harm, as we shall show, is literally life-threatening. At the same time, we recognize that a man cursing, degrading, and stripping his wife or girlfriend of her basic human dignity with words alone can also do serious damage. Moreover, much of the time physical abuse is accompanied by emotional and verbal violence as well.

Likewise, spanking is such a common way for parents to discipline children in America that it would be ridiculous for us to consider every paddling of a child as serious child abuse. Therefore, we have again taken the pragmatic route, defining child abuse as many shelter workers have: as severe physical discipline by a parent or caretaker by some means other than an open hand to the buttocks (for example, striking the child's body anywhere with implements such as belts, switches, kitchen utensils, extension cords, paddles, or feet). At the same time there is the additional problem of separating *abuse* from *neglect*. We agree with Naomi F. Chase, who in her excellent book *A Child Is Being Beaten,* distinguishes between outright physical abuse and neglect:

> Child abuse is the deliberate and willful injury of a child by a caretaker—hitting, beating with a belt, cord or other implement, slamming against a wall, burning with cigarettes, scalding with hot water, locking in a dungeon, hog-tying, torturing, even killing. It involves active hostile, aggressive physical treatment. Child neglect is more passive negative treatment characterized by a parent or custodian's lack of care and interest, and includes not feeding, not clothing, not looking after, not nurturing. The legal definitions vary in different states: so does the degree of harm done to the child.[7]

Taking this narrow physical definition of child abuse does not mean that we will totally ignore emotional injury to children resulting from the (sometimes savage) violence of their parents, or simple neglect. Limiting our main attention to purely physical types of abuse eliminates an enormous amount of conflict and injuries to family members. At the same time we believe it will lend the facts to be presented even greater credibility precisely because we have removed more subjective forms of abuse and limited our study to more unambiguous, clear-cut cases of conflict.

We hope that the patterns of violence uncovered will have an impact on the holders of power in our society who can legislate, allocate funds, and enforce statutes. At the present time relatively few public officials other than those who must regularly confront family violence, such as the police, have much sense of how widespread the problem is or of how serious can be its consequences. (And the police, as we shall show, frequently lack a clear notion of what to do about it.)

THE "MYTH" OF FAMILY VIOLENCE

The existence of family violence is no myth, but there are myths still commonly believed about its causes. It is fashionable for conservative politicians and media evangelists, particularly those involved in the controversial social movement known as the New Christian Right, to blame current problems of the American family, particularly divorce, on a number of so-called societal "ills." For example, claiming a "pro-family" stance (as if all who disagree with him are "anti-family"), Baptist minister Jerry Falwell and a host of local imitators across the country have tried to explain the problems in the American family by pointing to external pressures supposedly threatening it. Falwell and his organization see a woman's free choice to have or not have an abortion, the campaign for women's equal civil rights, television, pornography, and a dark conspiracy of "secular humanists" as undermining the family and encouraging divorce and unhappiness in marriages. Women have developed unrealistic career aspirations, which freedom from unwanted pregnancies and the Equal Rights Amendment movement have encouraged, and high divorce rates are the result, according to Jerry Falwell, Phyllis Schlafly, and a number of right-wing congressmen.

Thus they believe that by lobbying for constitutional amendments banning abortions and putting prayer back into public schools and against the Equal Rights Amendment (and other legislation in its spirit) they will somehow restore the "ideal," conflict-free American family. They believe in this happy family as a historical reality and feel that it has begun to disintegrate in our fast-paced, permissive society.

This is the myth of family violence: that it is a product of forces and pressures coming from outside the family. We need not dwell on the sexist nature of such myths. However, the point is that by focusing attention on things outside the family, "analysts" like Falwell undoubtedly miss one of the most pervasive, destructive forces threatening it. This force does not arise from without but rather from within the family. *Violence is the real threat to the American family, and it is generated among family members.* It can be found among couples where one or both persons lack honest, effective communication skills and ways to control anger and frustration. It can be found in the still-prevalent traditional attitudes among men that violence is an acceptable means of settling marital disputes and that as heads of the household they essentially hold property rights over women and children. It is true that outside economic pressures or even increased emphasis in the mass media on sexual promiscuity and violence may accelerate the problem. But they do not cause it.

Therefore we must look inside the family unit, not outside it, to understand why violence occurs. The current reluctance of many officials to admit this, which we shall document in later chapters, rests on myths that can only serve as obstructions to taking a hard look at the real roots of the problem. By examining the family dynamics of violence we can better comprehend why, when confronted with aggravating outside pressures and home violence, some women are literally driven from their homes and marriages. This kind of analysis will also point to what can be done to contain, reduce, and (however idealistic it may sound) eliminate such violence. We believe that violence as a dimension of how men relate to mates and children is unacceptable, not only to our own personal values but also to the larger spirit of the Judeo-Christian tradition on which our country was founded. That there has been so much family violence in our history does not discredit this spirit any more than widespread sin refutes the ideals of religion.

To set the stage for our findings about family violence, however, it is worth briefly reviewing the histories of both woman-battering and child abuse and to examine what is known about battering men. This review will reveal two ironic, conflicting patterns: how venerable are our traditions of family violence, and at the same time how recent is public recognition of the social problem.

WOMAN-BATTERING: A PERSISTENT HISTORICAL REALITY

It is still the conventional or "common sense" belief of many persons that women's shelters are simply havens for irresponsible women who cannot make a success of their marriages. Unfortunately, this misperception is held even by important officials in government. During the 1980 presidential campaign, for example, one front-running candidate reportedly remarked that women's shelters were places for women to go who wanted to avoid doing their housework. This is a classic example of "blaming the victim," shifting the responsibility for a crime or misfortune away from the real cause to the immediate victim.[8] To take an even more extreme example: one psychiatrist concluded after analyzing only four women that battered women are sadomasochists (needing and enjoying abuse for sexual pleasure), instigators of their assaults (nagging and provoking men into anger), and exploitative, masculine, domineering rivals (compulsively competing with males).[9]

Blaming the victim happened frequently during the 1960s when neo-racists tried to pinpoint the causes of black poverty in alleged inherent personality or even genetic traits. It continues to this day in the case of women who are raped and then accused of having invited sexual attack or even of unconsciously desiring it. It is a politically cheap way of doing little to address the real source of a problem but to look busy analyzing it. By a sometimes subtle and convincing logic, cause and effect are reversed and the victim is ironically transformed into the perpetrator of harm. Not all blaming of victims is done intentionally, of course. In the area of domestic violence, there is no

conspiracy of males or of social workers and therapists to promote it. But, as we shall show, there seems to be evidence that
considerable research on family violence, done by perfectly com-
petent professionals with good intentions and sympathy for the
plight of abused women in particular, contains a blaming-the-
victim bias.

Feminists, historians, social scientists, and journalists have
drawn together enough historical evidence to show that the
practice of woman-battering is as old as society itself. It is sometimes tied to women's child-bearing responsibilities, for pregnancy (it is argued) requires a certain dependence of women
on men for protection and support. Or sexual inequality (of
which woman-battering is only one form) has been thought of
as part of a bargain that women long ago struck with men
under unfair pressure. Feminist author Margaret Gates, for example, maintains that traditionally a wife was cherished and
protected (particularly from ravishings by other men) by a husband in exchange for her loyalty and submission to him, with
a beating her punishment for failing to keep her part of the
contract.[10] Whichever explanation one prefers, the inescapable
fact is that with a few exceptions women throughout history
have disproportionately been victims of violence and exploi-
tation.

Only in the last century has woman-battering been viewed
as a problem at all, much less as a serious problem. Two Scot-
tish sociologists traced the evolution of how wife-beating has
been viewed in the west since the days of the Roman Empire
and concluded:

> It has only been a hundred years since men were denied
> the legal right to beat their wives in Britain and the United
> States. Prior to the late 19th century it was considered a
> necessary aspect of a husband's marital obligation to con-
> trol and chastise his wife through the use of physical force.
> The legal prescriptions which once supported this practice
> no longer exist yet the behaviour continues unabated. Be-
> haviour which was once legally condoned is now proscribed

by law, yet cultural and normative prescriptions still support such practice and it is only mildly condemned, if at all, by law enforcement and judicial institutions . . .[11]

The Roman legacy that justified men subordinating women in marriages, shared undoubtedly by most of the civilized ancient world, continued into Christianity. The early Christian apostle Paul has become notorious among modern feminists for his advice to early Christians that placed women in a secondary role. For example, he cautioned:

Let your women keep silence in the churches: for it is not permitted unto them to speak; but they are commanded to be under obedience, as also saith the law.
And if they will learn any thing, let them ask their husbands at home: for it is a shame for women to speak in the church. (I Corinthians 14: 34–35)

In fact, Saint Paul explicitly advocated celibacy over matrimony, for marriage entangled men in the petty business of paying attention to women rather than to God:

He that is unmarried careth for things that belong to the Lord, how he may please the Lord:
But he that is married careth for the things that are of the world, how he may please his wife. (I Corinthians 7: 32–33)

Through the Roman Catholic church this biblically supported view made its way into European society and law. The idea of a man managing and controlling his family, disciplining both wife and children by right if in his opinion they deserved it, found fertile soil for acceptance. For many centuries, during the Dark and Middle Ages as well as the Renaissance, women were routinely subjugated. The physical punishment that accompanied their accepted inferior status, justified by the so-called "laws of chastisement," went unquestioned, though today we would consider it abuse. Such violence was simply taken for granted as part of the divinely ordained order of things.

> Accompanying these moral imperatives [of the Church] were the many laws of chastisement. During the Middle Ages women throughout Spain, Italy, France and England could be flogged through the city streets, exiled for years or killed if they committed adultery or numerous "lesser" offenses. In France a man could beat his wife, "when she contradicts or abuses him, or when she refuses, like a decent woman, to obey his reasonable commands" ... Even the French code of chivalry specified that the husband of a scolding wife could knock her to the earth, strike her in the face with his fist and break her nose so that she would always be blemished and ashamed. Thus, "the wife ought to suffer and let the husband have the word, and be the master" ...[12]

The sixteenth-century Protestant Reformation did little to improve the social position of women in Christan Europe. Early Protestants such as Martin Luther, John Knox, and John Calvin were as sexist as their Roman Catholic male contemporaries when it came to disciplining women physically. Journalist Terry Davidson cites a statement by Luther who, in boasting of his successful marriage, noted that when his wife occasionally became "saucy" all she received was a "box on the ear." [13]

This attitude of permissiveness toward striking women became a part of the American tradition through the original colonies' wholesale borrowing of much of English law. (Massachusetts was an exception. There, men who beat their wives in 1655 were fined a maximum of ten pounds and/or given corporal punishment.) An example was the now-infamous "rule of thumb," an expression that has become a part of our everyday speech. As Terry Davidson describes it:

> One of the reasons nineteenth century British wives were dealt with so harshly by their husbands and by their legal system was the "rule of thumb." Included in the British Common Law was a section regulating wifebeating. The

law was created as an example of compassionate reform
when it modified the weapons a husband could legally use
in "chastising" his wife. The old law had authorized a husband to "chastise his wife with any reasonable instrument."
The new law stipulated that the reasonable instrument be
only "a rod not thicker than his thumb." [14]

For a long time the battering of women was simply understood and accepted as a male's right in American society, though
it was not a statute or formal privilege. The Supreme Court of
Mississippi was the first to formalize the right in 1824. Other
courts in other states soon followed this trend, giving wife-
beating legal protection. Ironically, enshrining the right to
batter a woman in law was probably the beginning of the end
of its official protection, for once made part of the law, private
problems and vices invariably become open to public debate
and challenge. By the 1870s courts in states as different as Massachusetts and Alabama began rejecting the legal justification
of wife-beating. The pendulum began to swing the other way
as this "legitimate discipline" became viewed as cruelty. His-
torian Elizabeth Pleck notes that many states began adopting
quite harsh punishment for abusers (certainly more severe punishment than most such men now face):

A wifebeater, according to the Maryland law of 1882, could
receive forty lashes or one year in prison. . . In Delaware he
was punished with five to thirty lashes at the whipping
post, and in New Mexico with a fine of $255 to $1000 or
one to five years in prison . . .[15]

By 1910 only eleven states still did not permit divorce by reason of cruelty by one spouse to the other.
    This anti-abuse trend followed, or overlapped with, a similar
movement in England. There, "Speeches were made in the
House of Commons to the effect that, 'the country should treat
its married women no worse than it treated its domestic animals . . .' " [16] One of the most influential intellectuals and writ-

ers of the day, John Stuart Mill, passionately denounced wife-beating in his famous work, *The Subjection of Women*:

> However brutal a tyrant she may be chained to—though she may know that he hates her, though it may be his daily pleasure to torture her, and though she may feel it impossible not to loathe him—he can claim from her and enforce the lowest degradation of a human being, that of being made the instrument of an animal function contrary to her inclinations... When we consider how vast is the number of men, in any great country, who are little more than brutes, and that this never prevents them from being able, through the laws of marriage, to obtain a victim, the breadth and depth of human misery caused in this shape alone by the abuse of the institution swells to something appalling.[17]

Hearings were held by the British Parliament. In 1853 it passed the Act for Better Prevention and Punishment of Aggravated Assaults Upon Women and Children. While this certainly did not eliminate the problem, it was one of many steps taken toward at least removing the legal sanctioning of woman-battering, recognizing the dangers of such abuse to the family, and admitting that such violence was fundamentally immoral.

Rescinding laws legalizing abuse of women did not end the problem in the United States either. Nor was it eradicated by the women's suffrage movement in the early part of the twentieth century, the liberation of women from Victorian roles, the growing permissiveness about sexuality (in large part thanks to psychoanalyst Sigmund Freud), or the employment of large numbers of women in industry during World War II. It was only after the end of the Korean War that the first stirrings of a new, more concentrated attack on the problem of abuse could be felt.

Our awareness of it as a serious modern problem has come from several different sources. Various facts began accumulating in fairly unspectacular places that were eventually to become fuel for the movement. For example, criminologist Marvin E. Wolfgang published his often-cited article entitled simply "Husband-Wife Homicides" in 1956, pointing out that in a study of 588 homicides the ratio of wives killed by husbands to husbands killed by wives was four to one.[18] Then rape studies began to multiply, the frequent connection between woman-battering and child abuse in the same family was repeatedly noted by social workers, and—undoubtedly most important—the feminist movement began to cry out to persons concerned about the environment, the Vietnam War, and the civil rights movement for equal attention to uniquely female problems. By the early 1970s more and more professionals, mostly in the social service and counseling professions, began to communicate in publications and at conferences about mutual interests in female clients' problems. In 1976 the first White House Conference on Domestic Violence was held. States began holding public hearings on domestic violence, almost always spurred on by women's advocacy groups such as the National Organization for Women. Erin Pizzey, the founder of the battered women's shelter movement in Great Britain and the founder of the shelter movement worldwide, wrote *Scream Quietly or the Neighbors Will Hear,* while psychologist Lenore E. Walker wrote *The Battered Woman,* undoubtedly the most cited book ever written on woman abuse.[19] Soon momentum had built, and the body of work we present in the bibliography at the end of this book began to form.

What do we know and understand today of woman-battering? In some ways we know a great deal, but in others not as much as might appear at first glance. Statistics have been compiled on an ad hoc, uncoordinated basis across the nation, and often they sit unexamined in the files of social service agencies or state bureaucracies. Many of the persons whose job it is to collect and tally these figures are untrained or uninterested in analyzing them. As a result, conventional wisdom, subjectivity, and lack of a larger view still color much of what is published on the subject. Many studies are handicapped by using very small samples of women, making any sort of statistical analyses unconvincing.

Sociologists have collected a good deal of the statistical data. For instance, Murray A. Straus, Richard J. Gelles, and Suzanne K. Steinmetz conducted the first national study of randomly selected families, asking extensive questions about violence in the home among siblings, between spouses, and among generations. Their finding that 28 percent of the families reported some form of violence is highly significant, especially considering all the reasons respondents might have had for not being frank during interviews, for it means that at the very least almost one third of American families have experienced the violence problem.[20] If nothing else, it has contributed independent confirmation of the claims made by more individualistically (clinically) oriented professionals working in the front lines of social service agencies and shelters that woman-battering is tragically widespread.

Sociologists have also amassed an amazing assortment of statistical knowledge that in the future can be worked into the training of family counselors, police, and even architects. For example, Richard J. Gelles analyzed the "ecology" of marital violence (in which most of the more seriously injured victims were women) and found, among other things, that:

- The typical location of marital violence is the kitchen. The bedroom and living room are the next most likely scenes of violence.
- The bedroom is the most likely place for a female to be killed. Here conflicts often occur at night, when there is no place to go.
- The bathroom is the most frequently occupied room during domestic violence. Says Gelles, "The demilitarized zone of the home is the bathroom . . . The bathroom, typically the room in the house that *always* has a lock, is often used as a refuge for family members to hide in to avoid violence."

- Marital couples most often engage in physical conflict between 8:00 P.M. and 11:30 P.M.
- Marital violence is more frequent when neither spouse works, or when they work on alternating shifts.
- "Dinnertime is a particularly dangerous time due to the accumulation of frustration by the end of the day... the frustration builds to a crescendo during dinnertime as the wife complains about her day, the husband complains about his day, and the children yell, cry, spill or throw their food, and generally disrupt the dinner."
- Weekends are more conducive to domestic violence than weekdays.
- Holidays such as Christmas or New Year's Eve are notable "trouble times." [21]

Statistics have one advantage over more personalized, clinical studies in that they can reveal patterns which, if interpreted accurately, expand our understanding and refine our impressions of more qualitative findings. Many times persons who do research with and without statistics become antagonists and dispute the truth of each other's research due to their different approaches. This antagonism is unfortunate, since more is gained by combining skills than by quarrelling over strategies. As sociologists, we hope to bridge the problems of both approaches by interweaving our statistical data from the largest sample of battered women yet studied with the human side of the problem, drawn from anecdotes taken from our interviews with battered women in shelters other than the two we studied. Statistics are, of necessity, static; individual case studies are dynamic and reveal process. We believe there is no reason why a sociological study cannot show both.

CHILD ABUSE: A PERSISTENT
HISTORICAL REALITY

Children who are abused sexually, physically, and emotionally have one advantage over women who are abused—nobody blames the victim when it comes to violence against a child. Nobody accuses children who have been bruised, kicked, punched, scalded, mutilated, made into human pin cushions or ashtrays for lighted cigarettes, and starved by parents of being masochistic. Our awareness of this grotesque problem is only slightly older than that of woman-battering, but like woman-battering it appears to have a considerable history. Enough research has been collected on the legal codes and customs of past cultures to see that what we would consider family violence was formerly fairly common. For example, in Roman society the father's rights under the law included killing or maiming a son or daughter as well as sacrificing them to the gods. The father could also sell them as slaves if he wanted to.[22] The concept of children having rights, not only rights similar to those of adults but also special ones because of their vulnerability as children, is a modern one and certainly would have seemed foreign and even outrageous to the Romans. The plight of children in that ancient civilization had much in common with their lot during the next eighteen centuries.

The Bible is filled with gory stories of infanticide and violence toward children. Aside from examples such as God commanding Abraham to sacrifice his son Isaac (an order fortunately rescinded when Abraham passed the loyalty test), there are many instances of outright child slaughter, from Pharaoh's order to slay all Hebrew male infants at the time of Moses' birth to God's later act of taking the lives of all Egyptian firstborn to Herod's notorious Slaughter of the Innocents during Jesus' first days on earth.

Although denounced by the prophets, the sacrifice of firstborn sons was ordinary enough in ancient Palestine. The Book of Chronicles specifically names the Moabite King Mesha, who burned his eldest son for the god Chemosh; the Ammonites, who offered their sons to the Moloch; the Arameans, who sacrificed their children; and Ahaz and Manasseh [as killers of their children].

... The practice of child immolation was so common in ancient Israel that some scholars think Hell was the name originally given to Gehenna or Ge-Hinnom, the valley near Jerusalem where children were sacrificed. The valley, which was later turned into a garbage dump that burned continuously, has ever since been a literary image for the fires of Hell.[23]

As did the colonial settlers in this country, one can even read religious *support* for violence directed at children in the Old Testament:

He who spares his rod hates his son, but he who loves him disciplines him diligently. (Proverbs 13:24)

Do not hold back discipline from the child: although you beat him with the rod, he will not die.

You shall beat him with the rod, and deliver his soul from Sheol. (Proverbs 23:13–14)

Done today in the spirit of loving discipline or not, let the nearest child protective services office or a school nurse know you are beating a child with a rod and watch what happens! The movement to establish for children the right to be safe from physical and sexual abuse is relatively young. In this country it began just after the Civil War. Interestingly, the case that helped the movement gain visibility and momentum involved the Society for the Prevention of Cruelty to Animals. A little girl named Mary Ellen had to be taken from her family because in addition to being frequently beaten, she had been seriously neglected and became malnourished. There were no social service agencies for children who could argue in court on her behalf, so the Society for the Prevention of Cruelty to Animals maintained that as a member of the animal kingdom she should be removed from her abusive parents as was any animal's right by law. The society won its case. The obvious need for an entirely separate advocate to safeguard children, emphasized in large part by Mary Ellen's case, led to the formation of the Society for the Prevention of Cruelty to Children in 1871 in New York City.[24]

With the growing awareness that child violence and neglect, however sordid, were widespread enough to merit special attention, and as a greater sensitivity to the special needs of children emerged in such forms as child labor laws in the early part of the twentieth century, different states began requiring professionals who became aware of child abuse to report it. Today all fifty states have such laws. In 1974 Congress passed the Child Abuse Prevention and Treatment Act, which addressed sexual, physical and emotional abuse as well as neglect of persons under the age of 18 by their parents or guardians, strengthening official commitment to protecting children. This law was partly the result of events that took place as recently as 1960. In that year the term "battered child syndrome" was introduced by a physician, Dr. C. Henry Kempe, at a symposium for the American Academy of Pediatricians. Closer monitoring of hospital emergency rooms and increased awareness among physicians, social workers, and schoolteachers produced alarming evidence throughout the 1960s that child abuse was more frequent than previously suspected. Thus, lobbyists for various professional groups went to work, trying to convince Congress of the need for more protective laws concerning children.

As in the case of woman-battering, the figures on the extent of child abuse are often rough estimates, for much child abuse is never reported or is covered up by the abusers. Many times the victims are too young to tell anyone outside the home, or to leave. In the case of reporting child abuse there is also the problem that both parents can conspire to hide the maltreatment even if only one is directly abusing the young person. Sociologist David Gil is the preeminent researcher on the subject in social science. He estimated in 1965 that there were anywhere from 2.5 million to 4 million abused children in the United States. Critics quickly charged he had greatly exaggerated the problem, but a recent official study published by the U.S. Department of Health and Human Services pushed the figures of *known* child abuse incidents back toward the levels Gil had suggested. The National Center on Child Abuse and

Neglect reported in that study that their estimate of 652,000 [per year in the United States] abused and neglected American children was a bare minimum number. They believe that the actual incidences of child abuse and neglect are substantially greater than 652,000. In a footnote, the report followed this figure with another estimate: "Very likely, the actual number of children abused and neglected annually in the U.S. is at least 1,000,000." [25]

The statistics from agencies grossly underestimate the problem. Only the most severe cases, in the range of 60,000 to 75,000 per year, tend to get reported. Neighbors may know abuse is occurring but not want to intrude into another family's affairs. There are still too many persons who feel that what goes on in another's home is none of their business, no matter how violent it is. Some professionals, such as school nurses or teachers, may be reluctant to report suspected abuse for fear of a lawsuit if the abuse is not proven or if they believe their supervisors in the educational hierarchy will not back them. Other professionals may be pessimistic that much good will come out of reporting such violence, particularly if it is not extreme, for they may feel some mistaken responsibility to keep the family together at the expense of bruises on the child. Or they may know that unless a child is severely injured or killed, and unless a district attorney's office will prosecute the case, proven abuse will not be considered a criminal offense any more than it is for women who are beaten at home.

Initially we did not set out to include children in this study of domestic violence. We thought that looking at abuse of children would only complicate the issue and had decided that we would stick to the topic of battered women, narrowly but thoroughly analyzing their predicament. This proved to be impossible. As we shall show, most abused women who come to a shelter for help bring children with them, and many of these children are also victims of abuse. In fact, one of the most noticeable impressions of a women's shelter is the large number of children and the frequent din of them playing, laughing, and crying. In our research we came to recognize that the children were inseparable from their mother's plight, that they were part of it as well as being victims themselves. Family violence, we saw, had a number of destructive consequences for children, even when they were not beaten. Thus not only their presence, but their problems as well, are a critical part of the reality of a women's shelter. For that reason we will devote some effort to reporting the effects of family violence on children.

THE BATTERER

So far we have given an overview of the victims of violent family environments. However, our concern in this book is with the total family, and therefore we include an analysis of the perpetrators of violence in the home. In most cases this is a legal husband, though it may be a boyfriend or ex-husband of a woman.

At the present time there is no definitive information on the batterer. He is usually the invisible villain in most studies. There is little known about the motives of the batterer, his presumed need to dominate another person through physical force, or how he feels after a violent act. Much of our so-called "understanding" of the batterer is really only arm-chair speculation. For example, some psychologists view the batterer as a male child that was taught to be aggressive, either directly or indirectly. He is believed to have been rewarded for behaving that way, raised feeling that such behavior is appropriate for males in general. For example, psychologist Lenore Walker states in the introduction to her book *The Battered Woman*:

> Perhaps when more is known about batterers, we will need to view them also as victims. Certainly those whom I have known did not commit their crimes without severe psychological distress. They, too, are caught in a bind placed upon them by their socialized need to maintain dominance.[26]

We recognize the importance of child-rearing in the development of each personality, but pragmatically speaking we find it difficult to think of the abuser as a victim, especially after encountering the grotesque physical and psychological damage that he inflicts so often on his wife and/or children. From a scientific point of view, the fact that the male abuser might himself have been beaten as a child must be established, not merely assumed, and if established, then related back to his adult behavior. It may be, as we suspect, that regarding every adult as the automatic product or end result of his or her upbringing is too simple an explanation for adult violence. In the case of the violent male, this approach lets everyone off the hook—in other words, everybody, including the abuser, becomes transformed into a victim. Therefore nobody is really personally at fault (except some vaguely defined "socializers" or parents, who are no longer around to blame), and thus what is often really a crime by any reasonable standards becomes "scientifically" redefined as the act of a person who is acting out his childhood conditioning.

In family relationships there often exists a high degree of intimacy, deep emotional involvement, and interaction. These are precisely the conditions that breed the most intense conflict, for conflict is often repressed in the name of intimacy, but when it does finally surface, it explodes. Society, by its ignorance or acceptance of family violence, has allowed the continual repetition of such a problem. To change matters would take a major realignment of attitudes and beliefs among both men and women. For example, Bonnie Carlson points out what would be involved in circumventing wife-beating as an accepted practice for men:

> As long as men believe that responding to stress and frustration with aggression or physical violence is acceptable behavior, the problem of the battered women will continue to exist. Thus, in addition to improving the ability of men and women to support themselves and their families, efforts should be made to eradicate the beliefs that: (1)

men's status must and should be higher than women's;
(2) men who are not dominant and are not physically more
powerful than women are in some way not masculine and
adequate; and (3) physical power and coercion are valid
means of solving disputes in the family or in any other
interpersonal relationships.[27]

Our research includes the largest number of (male) batterers
ever analyzed. Realistically, we cannot expect to resolve in one
study the mystery of why they often batter so compulsively or
so severely. However, we can use information on their backgrounds and activities to understand the effects of violence on
the family as a whole and to clarify the real dangers which face
not only family members but also other agents who must deal
with them, such as police officers. If our approach to the batterer seems sometimes insensitive or unsympathetic, it is because we are staunchly reacting against much of the professional
"conventional wisdom" that perceives batterers as passive victims of childhood abuse, which they automatically pass on,
rather than as assailants in the most criminal sense of the term.
There has been far too much psychological and sociological
determinism in accounting for why people do what they do.
Social forces do not batter women and children; conscious, free,
responsible men do. They know what they do, and research
shows that they can learn and choose not to batter.

THE FOCUS ON FAMILY VIOLENCE

Family violence is just that. It cannot be understood simply
as violence toward women and/or children. It involves all
members of the family, though it may affect them in different
ways. To look at just one of its aspects, such as its victims or
its perpetrators, cannot provide us with a complete picture of
the problem. Our goal is to contribute to a better picture of
this entire phenomenon, examining in the chapters to follow
all the actors in the tragedy of family violence. This will include not only the immediate members of the family but also

persons in the community who must confront the problem. Family violence regularly touches officials in the criminal justice system, family relatives, and friends, to name only a few who are involved. As we will see, they all play a role, however indirect, in the violent home. If there is any solution on the horizon, it will have to be one in which they are more directly concerned.

2
WOMEN: THE MOST VISIBLE VICTIMS

Nobody marries for worse. When a minister reads the final lines of what people hope is a lifelong commitment in the marriage ceremony, "for better or for worse," nobody imagines the second alternative: daily terrorization, bruised and scarred faces, damaged optic nerves, broken bones, acid poured on unprotected skin, stab wounds, gunshots, pistol-whippings, and rape. The same is true for those men and women living together in common-law households: their faces are turned toward the light, not the possible darkness, of the future. Yet in many instances, not long after the relationship commences the dark side begins to emerge. For example, here are the testimonies of two women at a Michigan public hearing:

> When I first got married, the beatings started about the first week that the rent didn't get paid. We got along for a couple more weeks, and then I wanted to go to a meeting that night and he thought that I shouldn't go, so then I got beaten for that. It was just one situation after another.

> I was married and within the first three days the battering began. . . I divorced my first husband and remarried, and it

was the same thing all over again. Within a couple of months the battering began again. The physical battering in the second marriage was just unbelievable. I began to feel that this was all there was to life—that there was no way out . . . There was an instance in the first marriage where I was five months pregnant, and I was grabbed around the waist and squeezed. My head was slammed against towel racks and into the top of the tank of the toilet, and the top of the tank broke in half. The baby lived . . . In the second marriage, my life was threatened and I believed it and knew it was possible. My eyes would be swollen shut for three weeks. I have been afraid of going to the doctor because of how people look at you when you start talking about it. I am just now healed up. There was one instance where my head was split open and I had to have stitches because my face was torn apart.[1]

Such accounts have been duplicated more than a thousand-fold in clinical interviews, police reports, testimonies in public hearings, published documents, and the files of the nation's battered women's shelters. We personally have listened to many of them in their horrifying detail. Yet many people at first cannot bring themselves to believe that such events actually occur daily across America or that such violence happens except in the homes of sadists and masochists. Even when they acknowledge that violence exists on a shockingly wide scale, the dynamics of such brutality often seem beyond comprehension. Eventually the question has to be asked: How can people live like that?

These incidents are actually not so mysterious. Violence against women by men in their own homes is not random behavior. It is patterned and understandable. We hope that this fact means that it can someday be controlled and eradicated. In this chapter we ask three important questions about women who are victims of family violence:

How severely are they hurt? Are these women truly justified in leaving their mates and lovers, at least temporarily, for sanctuary in havens supported (in part) by public tax dollars? To put it another way, do the rest of us, as taxpayers, really need to contribute monies to "bail out" these women from their personal marital difficulties? Are they only complainers, or are they truly women in desperate circumstances?

Who are these women? Are they women who are burned-out products of the new sexual equality, which pressures women to maintain a home and children and simultaneously keep a full-time job? Are they women who have forsaken raising children and therefore, as working wives, become threats or rivals to their spouses? Are they predominantly welfare mothers, minority women, or women with drug or alcohol problems? Are they women who were exposed to family violence as little girls, either as observers or victims?

Why did these women endure the abuse for as long as they did, and what made them decide to leave? This third question is the most frequently asked by the person unfamiliar with domestic violence: Why did these women not leave *immediately* once violence and injuries began? After all, don't they have opportunities to leave, preferable to facing an obviously unpleasant situation?

In answering each question, we will begin to explore the scope of family violence and the predicament of women caught up as the victims.

HOW SEVERELY ARE THEY HURT?

For women who manage to leave scenes of severe family violence and make their way to publicly supported shelters, sometimes escaping as if they had been kept prisoners in their own homes, it seems reasonable to ask how badly they have been abused. Are they simply poor homemakers, or do they have a legitimate claim to being physically endangered? Statistics can help us decide what we ought to make of such women. The numbers and percentages to follow may make our description seem cold-blooded at times, but remember that such figures stand for real persons and experiences. To that extent, they convey a certain horror above and beyond any individual account of violence, for they speak of many incidents, not a few isolated ones. This section should leave little doubt as to whether or not these women masochistically wanted to experience abuse (consciously or unconsciously) or whether they in any way deserved the violence they suffered.

The Ways Women Are Beaten

The 542 shelter residents in our study recounted an incredible variety of ways that they had been abused by the men in their homes. Often these men hurt them in more than just one way, throwing a barrage of different blows at the women. The most frequent combination of violence came in the form of slapping, punching, and kicking. For example, eight out of ten women were slapped, over seven out of ten were punched, and six out of ten were kicked. (See Table 2-1.)*

More serious abuse, some of it life-threatening, was not uncommon. In over 10 percent of the cases the man had done such things as crush out lighted cigarettes on the woman's back, neck, face, or arms, throw acid on her, or hold a butane lighter against her hair or body. These burning incidents seemed to us to come the closest to outright cruelty. For example, one husband poured a can of drain cleaner into his wife's open palm and forced her to hold her hand under the running kitchen faucet. Another husband drenched his wife's clothes with gasoline during an argument and stalked her through the house with matches, threatening to "torch" her.

Some abusers were what domestic violence experts call "pushers"—not drug dealers, but men whose style of violence is to shove the woman into walls, over furniture, or down stairs. Jerking a woman around by her hair or forcing her head down so that she was unable to see as she was pummelled were also common tactics of some men.

The violence often escalated. While half the women had been

---

* All tables are in Appendix A at the end of the book.

threatened with weapons, one out of five men actually used one during a beating. By weapons we mean (and the women meant) more than just a gun or knife. There were, of course, many women who had been stabbed, cut, shot, and pistol-whipped. But in family violence the definition of a weapon embraces a virtual inventory of household objects that otherwise might seem perfectly harmless. During our research we began keeping an unofficial tally of the weapons that women reported their men had used. This list, which obviously does not exhaust all the possible weapons in a household "arsenal" that could be used to hurt, included pistols, shotguns, knives, machetes, golf clubs, baseball bats, electric drills, high-heeled shoes, sticks, frying pans, electric sanders, toasters, razors, silverware, ashtrays, drinking glasses and beer mugs, bottles, burning cigarettes, hair brushes, lighter fluid and matches, candlestick holders, scissors, screwdrivers, ax handles, sledgehammers, chairs, bedrails, telephone cords, ropes, workboots, belts, door knobs, doors, boat oars, cars and trucks, fish hooks, metal chains, clothing (used to smother and choke), hot ashes, hot water, hot food, dishes, acid, bleach, vases, rocks, bricks, pool cues, box fans, books, and, as one woman described her husband's typical weapons, "anything handy."

Sometimes the weapons were used merely to intimidate the women. One case not from the shelters but from our independent interviews involved a husband who would sometimes wave a loaded revolver around the house in front of his wife and children. Then he would unpredictably creep up behind his wife while she was absorbed in washing dishes or cooking, suddenly put the barrel of the gun to her head, and pull the trigger on an empty chamber. He never shot her (that was to be her father's fate when he tried to prevent the armed husband from breaking into the parents' house intent on killing her), but the psychological terror such behavior created over a period of months and years undeniably exhausted her mental and physical health.

In other instances weapons were used with nearly homicidal

consequences. We listened to a story told by an attractive young mother whose abusive husband objected to the two-piece bathing suit she wore as they set out for an afternoon at the lake. She refused to change it and went to get in their pick-up truck despite his objections. In front of their preschool-age daughter, the husband waited as the wife crossed in front of the truck, then deliberately gunned the engine and rammed her against the back of the garage, pinning her to the wall by one leg. He shifted into reverse and drove away to a bar, leaving her to bandage her bleeding leg and drive herself to the hospital.

Battering of a pregnant woman is particularly shocking because of its frequency: 42 percent of the women in shelters report experiencing this. Usually it takes the form of a man slapping a woman or punching and kicking her in the vulnerable abdomen or genitals. There is good reason to suspect that this kind of violence is really aimed as much at harming the unborn child as at hurting the wife, as clearly illustrated by the example of one Dallas man who forced his wife to abort her fetus by making her drink bleach. Many researchers have observed the escalated hostility that pregnancy seems to bring out in batterers. They sometimes become literally murderous toward the unborn baby. The woman's pregnancy heightens the man's sense of jealousy and possessiveness, yet at the same time he seems to blame her for her impending motherhood. In many cases these men are terribly dependent on the woman, despite their bravado. The thought of a competitor fills them with dread. Psychologist Lenore Walker notes from her interviews with several hundred women:

> Most of the women interviewed said the physical violence became more acute during pregnancy and their child's infancy. Men who are dependent upon their women logically become frustrated when the woman begins to pay attention to dependent infants instead of to them. I suspect that is probably one of the reasons why violence increases during pregnancy. All of a sudden, the man is forced to share his woman with another person. In some cases, the women said

that they thought their men were attempting to prevent another human being that might have the same bad genes as himself from being born into the world. More often, it was a simple case of prenatal child abuse.[2]

Others have observed the same thing. Elaine Hilberman, a psychiatrist, and Kit Munson, a psychiatric nurse-consultant, at Chapel Hill, North Carolina, found in a study of sixty physically abused women who had been referred to a rural health clinic for psychiatric evaluation that

> changes in the pattern of violence during pregnancy were noted by most women. There was increasing abuse for some, the pregnant abdomen replacing face and breasts as the target for battering, with abortions and premature births the result.[3]

The crisis telephone calls to the Hotline at Dallas's Family Place, representing a large population of women who usually do not end up in a shelter, tell a similar story of women being battered while pregnant. Of the women calling in, 42 percent complained that they were physically abused during pregnancy, a grim indicator indeed for the larger picture of family violence. As the next section of this chapter will show, the backgrounds of these women make it likely that they will be at the peak of their child-bearing years when they first marry, and thus the chances that they will become pregnant at this time are maximized.

A final comment about the kinds of violence these women have endured puts the battering-during-pregnancy figure into clearer context and also suggests something about the sexual psychology of the batterer. One in four Dallas–Fort Worth Metroplex women in our study reported sexual abuse by their husbands or boyfriends when they were admitted to the shelters. Sexual abuse here includes rape (forcing the woman to have sexual intercourse or perform other sexual acts against her will, through threats or actual physical coercion), kicking or striking the woman in the genitals, and mutilating her breasts or genitals. Abuse can also take more subtle forms. One Hotline call involved a husband dressing in his wife's lingerie and then forcing her to make love to him. Lenore Walker devotes an entire chapter in her book *The Battered Woman* to the bizarre sexual tastes of many batterers, including bestiality with the family dog, domination, and sadism.[4] Our shelter statistics do not indicate the same extent of sexual abuse as Walker found (only 25 percent of the women reported it), and we would be content to let that be our conclusion were it not for an additional piece of information.

At one counseling session with a group of women, a Dallas shelter counselor was asked by one of the participants if sex problems could be discussed. Given encouragement to speak freely, the client began to describe how her husband had demanded sexual intercourse with her two to four times *daily*, accusing her of infidelity with other men, or of falling down in her marital responsibilities if she didn't feel "in the mood." He would become violent if she resisted or protested. Like many of the women in the group, this wife was in her first marriage and had married early in her adulthood. Consequently she had had little sexual experience with other men and was naive enough not to know whether his sex demands were unreasonable or not. She had begun to wonder if she was frigid, a possibility he would frequently raise.

Other women in the group spontaneously contributed similar stories, some telling how they had rationalized the man's excessive demands for sex by deciding that frequent, one-sided coitus was (at the worst) a way of draining off some of his tension, thus preventing other violence. Any refusal to have sex, or failure to comply with some other preference (such as oral or anal intercourse, or sex with multiple partners), would be grounds for beating her. Some women had begun to suspect that the man's demands for sexual experimentation were really covers for his fears of latent homosexuality. Since that serendipitous mentioning of the sex issue, the Dallas shelter women's experiences with sexual domination and the role of sexuality in their abuse is now more explicitly anticipated and dealt with, and it occurs in counseling discussions regularly.

Sexual domination to the point of abuse is also often interwoven with other forms of violence. For example, one woman testified at a public hearing:

> My husband hit me on his lawyer's advice. Several years before the incident, according to my husband, his lawyer had advised him that the best way to dominate a wife is by being sexually aggressive, and, if that failed, by beating her . . . I feel that my husband's violence was related to his need to hold power over people. He had held sexual power over me, but in the few months preceding these incidents, he had made it quite clear that he wanted a sexual parting, but not a divorce. If I thought he was adulterous, that just showed how depraved I was![5]

Thus, the figure of approximately one in four women reporting sex abuse probably underestimates the true level of such activity. Only after living at the shelter and sharing their intimate feelings and experiences do abused women begin to gain some outside standard for judging their past sexual lives as abusive. The role of marital rape—itself an as-yet poorly understood or legally defined phenomenon—in domestic violence is very likely suppressed by many women out of sheer ignorance that the sexual abuse they have known is anything different from what most women experience.

The Injuries Women Receive

We would expect high rates of injuries among these women. After all, a basic requirement for admission to a shelter in Texas is evidence or threat of physical danger to the woman. From what we have seen of how these women were abused, it would be very surprising if they did not have a high number of injuries.

In fact, most of the shelter women (83 percent) were visibly bruised when they arrived at the shelters, and close to half had been cut. Many were both. One woman in five had one or more broken bones when she came to the shelter. Some had faces so badly beaten that doctors had to wait for the swelling to subside before the bones could be set. The same proportion of pregnant women had complications with their pregnancies because of beatings. (See Table 2-2.)

One in three women in our study required medical treatment. Some women required continued treatment for twisted joints, sprained backs, or broken bones and jaws; bridge work to replace loosened teeth; and occasionally even plastic surgery. Yet shelters can provide no direct medical services. Instead, they must shuttle women with serious injuries back and forth to doctors, clinics, and hospitals. Often such women have contacted the shelter from a hospital emergency room after being driven there by a relative or friend. Still in pain, they there and then make up their minds not to return home.

We asked Eve McArthur, a former director of Austin's Center for Battered Women and currently executive associate director of the Texas Council on Family Violence, to recall from her experience on the shelter staff the most unforgettable adult victim of serious violence. She immediately described a woman who called from a hospital requesting placement in the shelter. Shelter staff members visited her at the hospital, finding a woman whose body and head were horribly bruised and swollen. Some time later, after the swelling and disfigurement had begun to recede, the woman was recovered enough to be released from the hospital. So grotesque had been the distortion of her normal features from pain and the results of her earlier beatings that when she showed up at the shelter to be admitted no one who had interviewed her in the hospital even recognized her.

Thus, despite cynicism from some who would like to wish away the severity of woman-battering or minimize the importance of women's shelters for alleviating real human misery, such places do provide a vital service for certain women. One could literally say that in some cases they provide a life-saving service.

WHO ARE THESE WOMEN?

All of the 542 Dallas–Forth Worth Metroplex women in this study had one thing in common: they all made the decision to leave their homes, at least temporarily, for their own physical safety and sometimes also that of their children. Beyond this common denominator, there are a number of other similarities in their backgrounds that we can identify. As we shall show, the women who eventually come to shelters are not a representative cross section of all abused women. For one thing, based on what other studies have found about domestic violence generally, we know that shelter residents (and applicants) are some of the more severely abused women. The level of abuse in many American homes, as in many Texas homes, is undoubtedly not yet severe enough to prompt some sufferers to leave. In addition, some women have more resources than others and thus can escape abuse in ways other than seeking sanctuary in a women's shelter. (Later we shall consider these resources.)

Their Current Characteristics

The background characteristics of the 542 female clients in the shelters in our study make some definite statements about the problems, needs, and resources that battered women present when they arrive at the shelters (see Table 2-3):

Age. These clients were relatively young women (the average age was 25), still in the years when family and home are usually being established. Most women brought at least two young children with them when they entered the shelter; many were pregnant with another child. (Only 16 percent had no children.)

Marital background. The majority of the women were married when they entered shelters, and of these the majority were in their first marriage.

Ethnic background. The majority of the shelter residents were white, with one in five black, one in ten Spanish-speaking, and a small percentage native American, Oriental, or another group. The United States census statistics show similar proportions in the Dallas–Fort Worth population. Thus it appears that family violence is not the monopoly of any one specific ethnic group with alleged traditions of violence.

Education. A slight majority of these women were high school graduates and some had taken some college courses. Very few had college degrees. Four out of ten women did not have a high school education.

Income/occupation. Economically, these women can best be described as lower-middle and lower class. Almost half of the women worked outside the home but earned less than $10,000 a year. One fourth of these had specific job skills; most, however, worked at low-paying, unskilled jobs. But the majority of the women had no jobs outside of being full-time homemakers. Contrary to stereotypes often portrayed by politicians and the media, we found that few of the shelter residents had been receiving Aid to Families with Dependent Children when they entered the shelters and even fewer were receiving other supplemental welfare payments.

These facts explain why only two out of three women had any money when they arrived at a shelter. Most who did brought less than $50 with them. Most of these women did not have jobs or incomes separate from those of their husbands or boyfriends. Certainly those who earned some income did not have enough money for them and their children to live on.

What sort of average portrait emerges from the patterns uncovered? We may answer this question in part by pointing out what these women were not. They were not the indigent (disproving the stereotype of battered women or shelter residents as welfare mothers or "career welfare recipients"), nor were they predominantly minority women. They were not representative of all ages—rather, for the most part they were young mothers. They did not show histories of numerous divorces.

Moreover, we found that very few had either alcohol or drug-related problems. Significantly, they were not middle- and upper-class. These women did not have jobs paying a living wage even when they did work outside the home. In many cases their limited educations put them at a clear disadvantage in a labor market increasingly demanding greater skills and training and higher levels of formal education. (Later we will see that the average income of the batterers, on which a majority of the women had to rely, was low as well.)

This lower-income portrait of the battered woman differs from the results of some of the early research by clinical psychologists who were more likely to come in contact with middle- and upper-class women through their private practices.[6] At the same time, our findings do not prove or suggest what some sociologists call "the class myth" of family violence. This myth states that such violence is largely confined to lower-class homes and is a product of a violent subculture shared by such families. It is true that lower-class families are most affected by economic and social strains and frustrations. They are more likely to live in crowded, less comfortable homes or apartments, with fewer conveniences and more children. When the overall economy declines, these families suffer first and longest. All past studies, using either official statistics or figures generated independently, have found higher rates of violence among lower-class families. But a large number of studies now show that domestic violence, particularly woman-battering, is nevertheless found throughout all levels of American society. George Levinger, for example, found in one study of divorces that one in four middle-class women reported physical abuse as one reason for ending her marriage. Another study, by John O'Brien, found that 15 percent of 150 couples, half of whom were middle-class, obtaining divorces brought up overt violence spontaneously as one reason they wanted their marriages dissolved. Sociologists Rodney Stark and James McEvoy III randomly sampled 1176 Americans and discovered not only that one in five approved of slapping one's spouse if he/she "deserved it" but also that such approval was found in middle- as well as in lower-income families.[7]

The key reason our study contains so many lower- and lower-middle-class women comes down to the basic matter of resources. People without resources generally appear in public statistics, whether police records, unemployment rolls, mental hospital admission lists, or bureaucratic records on domestic violence, because they have little choice. Women without separate incomes or well-paying jobs or the educational qualifications to find work, plus the responsibilities of caring for small children, find few alternatives when they feel they must get out of their homes in order to be safe. A night in a motel is not cheap anywhere, even in a bargain motel. Approximately 70 percent of the women in our study do not have access to transportation, even through friends or neighbors. (The Dallas–Fort Worth region is typical of many urban areas in having minimal public transportation. The city of Denton, Texas, for example, does not even have a single taxicab.)

People can also be thought of as resources. Many women resort to relying on relatives to put them up for a day or two, but as we shall show in the next section, most of the shelter residents have been beaten repeatedly for many months and often for years. The hospitality and patience of friends, neighbors, and relatives runs out after a point, particularly if there is a violent, furious man literally stalking the woman and ready to punish her for "running out on him." It is not unusual for those who give the women shelter to be threatened themselves. Women we talked with could not always rely even on close relatives. Parents often disapprove of the daughter's marriage to the batterer in the first place, making her return to them an unpleasant series of I-told-you-so's. Or, they may blame her for not making the marriage work.

In-laws also are often of little help. Mothers-in-law frequently told these women, when they complained of abuse, "Y what kind of man he was before you married h your bed, so lie in it." Or the in-laws took the blaming the woman for provoking him. "They said I must be some kind of bitch to rile him up so," one shelter resident reported. Nor was the church always a sympathetic place to turn. Several women bitterly complained to us how they had gone to ministers or priests and been given the same basic message: "You married for better or worse. This is simply the other side of the coin, the 'worse' part, and you must endure it." One young woman, a former Southern Baptist who had been divorced several years prior to marrying her battering husband, was even told by her preacher that her beatings were God's punishment for dissolving her first marriage! Even the Salvation Army, traditionally a refuge for down-and-out persons, can do little beyond providing temporary shelter (often for only a few days) for a relatively tiny number of women and children. The Salvation Army Center in Dallas, for instance, is the agency where Family Place most commonly sends women for temporary shelter when it is full (which is almost always), yet as of May 1, 1982, the Center reportedly had spent *all* of its 1982 budget in responding to the tidal wave of applicants.

Thus it is not surprising that resource-poor women should make up most of the clientele of shelters. In contrast, we do have some idea of how middle- and upper-middle-class women cope with abuse. Dallas' Family Place operates a Help Center, an outreach program aimed primarily at middle-class women who do not necessarily wish (or need) to move out of their homes or end their marriages. Many of these women have professional jobs, good education, high incomes, and, aside from occasional physical violence, comfortable homes. They can afford to establish separate living arrangements in apartments or townhouses, take lovers, or hide out at health spas and country clubs. The impact of family violence on their lives is certainly not pleasant, but they are usually not in such desperate economic straits when violence occurs. A woman who is the wife of a lawyer, doctor, or executive earning $150,000 a year, who has a maid or other servants, a beautiful house, her own ʼr, and checking and charge accounts is in a very different situation when she confronts domestic violence from a young woman with two or more small children, no high school diploma, no job, little cash, and no car. Battered women's shelters see more of the latter type of woman by default, because she has run out of other options.

Their Experiences of Past Family Violence

Many psychologists, social workers, and sociologists have claimed that children who are exposed to violence grow up to become violent adults, both as mates and as parents. This concept is generally known as the "generational transfer hypothesis." Here we want to see how it applies to women; in Chapter four we will test it on batterers.

Logically, the generational transfer hypothesis can operate in two ways. First, children imitate their parents' behavior and indirectly learn what is "appropriate," what is rewarding, and what works in family arguments. Such imitation, furthermore, can produce different results in males and females. From watching their fathers, boys can learn that violence is a successful tactic for winning compliance from women. It achieves definite goals, such as cooperation, sex, and silence. It apparently wins arguments. Moreover, it is "manly." From watching their mothers, girls can learn that being beaten is part of a female's normal lot in life as beating is a male's prerogative. The hypothesis also operates in a second way. Being beaten as a child implicitly teaches that child the normality of being beaten by those who are supposed to love him or her. Intimacy and violence thus become fused. Violence is also learned as an appropriate tactic for controlling family members. It can be incorporated into the personality as a deep-seated, aggressive reaction to frustration (as with many men) or as a factor encouraging passive responses (as with many women).

The three sociologists who conducted the largest survey on family violence to date succinctly sum up these two aspects of the generational transfer hypothesis:

> Each generation learns to be violent by being a participant
> in a violent family . . . Generally, those who grow up in
> homes in which parents were violent to each other tended
> to be violent to each other in their own marriages . . . Par-
> ents who were subjected to a great deal of physical punish-
> ment have the highest rates of abusive violence toward
> their own children.[8]

Their findings indicate that this inheritance of violence is
strongest in families where children not only see their parents
use violence on each other but are also victims of violence from
parents: "When a child grows up in a home where parents use
lots of physical punishment and also hit each other, the chances
of becoming a violent husband, wife or parent are greatest of
all." [9]

This kind of conclusion is by no means rare. For example,
an independent study in Michigan conducted by a social worker
summed up its results as follows:

> There was a direct relationship between being a victim or
> an assaulter in the present situation and having been wit-
> ness to parental violence in one's childhood. There was also
> a relationship to having been victims of child abuse them-
> selves.[10]

Undeniably, children imitate adults and learn styles of family interaction. Unfortunately, many of the conclusions such
as those just presented, regardless of how statistically precise they
are or how large the sample used, are based on the worst type
of social science information: retrospective data, which in many
cases goes back to respondents' early childhoods. Because no
one was actually there making independent observations on
how current adults were raised and what types of violence they
were exposed to, social scientists are forced to ask respondents
what they can recall about what they, as children, understood
about their parents' interaction and child-rearing styles. The
potential for distortion, selective memory, and exaggeration of

harsh discipline by parents is serious, particularly if the respondent is being interviewed in a situation where he or she is very sensitive to the violence issue. Since most psychologists, social workers, and social psychologists believe in the predominant role of early learning for explaining what adults become, it is natural for them to look for the roots of adult violence in childhood experiences.

However, as social worker Srinika Jayaratne stated in a review of the research on the generational transfer hypothesis, the link between supposed childhood exposure to violence and adult experience with it is not that well established scientifically, particularly since most of the findings come from special subpopulations, such as small groups of severely abused women. Jayaratne claims that the generational phenomenon of child abuse is one of the most commonly held conceptions (or misconceptions) about abusing parents.[11]

Some studies find the instances of exposure to parental violence among current victims of abuse by spouses nowhere near as common as is often thought. For example, Hilberman and Munson, in their in-depth analysis of 60 battered women referred to a rural health clinic, reported:

> Life-long violence was the pattern for many of these women, who gave remarkably similar histories. Violence between parents, usually the father assaulting the mother, paternal alcoholism, and the physical and/or sexual abuse of these women as children *were described by half the women*.[12] (Italics ours.)

In other words, the battered women were just as likely *not* to have been exposed to violence directed by one parent at another or at them. Similarly, Bruce J. Rounsaville found that only one in four battered women in his studies had been abused as children.[13] Another important study of abused women by sociologist Mildred Daley Pagelow also found no overwhelming evidence for the generational transfer hypothesis.[14] Studies such as these challenge this hypothesis as a "neat" explanation for why women stay in abusive relationships or why they find themselves in currently violent circumstances.

We will examine current rates of child abuse in battered women's families in the next chapter and reasons women reported for staying in violent relationships in the next section. Here we are trying to establish if, in the opinions of shelter residents themselves, they were victims of violence and neglect as children. Unfortunately, there is the real possibility that these women might exaggerate past violence in their lives, to get sympathy or because they become sensitive to any kind of harsh discipline after coming to a shelter. Alternatively, many of these women might have come from homes where violence was so commonplace and accepted that they recall nothing remarkable about their parents' disciplining of them or each other. For the time being we will have to contend with all the problems inherent in using retrospective, autobiographical information, and trust that the different causes of memory distortion cancel each other out. At least if these women do *not* uniformly report past childhood violence we will know they are not exaggerating their past victimization.

We asked shelter residents for their recollections of their parents' relations to one another and to them, and for their estimation of their mothers' and fathers' possible problems with alcohol. Their responses reveal a clear pattern: one woman in three witnessed violence between her parents, one in four felt she was abused as a child, one in five felt she had been neglected, one in ten felt her mother had an alcohol problem, and between one woman in three and one in four felt her father had an alcohol problem. In other words, there is evidence of previous experience with violence in some of these women's lives, but it is certainly not a compelling explanation for their current problems. (See Table 2-4.)

Since only a small percentage of the shelter women experienced abuse and/or neglect as children we decided to look more carefully at the types and extent of violence in their present family situations. We combined the form of violence (such as slaps, punches, kicks) with the type of injury (bruises, cuts, broken bones) to construct an index of the severity of violence within a woman's present family environment (see Appendix B for a more detailed discussion of the family violence Severity Index). If the generational transfer hypothesis is true, the combined effect of the form(s) of battering and type(s) of injury should give higher scores for women who have been raised in a violent home environment. We found that the evidence for this theory is at best weak for battered women. Slightly more women who were abused or neglected as children scored higher on this index than women not experiencing family violence as children, but these differences cannot be considered large enough in a statistical sense to support the hypothesis. (Other factors, such as violence between a woman's parents, a woman's education, or her having or not having a job, also have little effect on the forms of battering she was willing to endure or the extent of injury resulting from these attacks. Finally, we found that women who experienced severe battering in a previous relationship were less likely to endure severe battering in a second.)

In summary, childhood exposure to violence had no detectable effect on those women who experienced it, *and most did not.* Thus we rule out childhood abuse or neglect and seeing parents' violence as important overall causes of the women's adult abuse. We reject generalizations such as one in a popular book on the subject of domestic violence (which reflects many conventional ideas):

> Young girls may grow up thinking that men are supposed to hit their wives, and such role expectations may become the incentive for their husbands to use violence on them. And women who have been raised in violent homes are more likely to marry men who are prone to use violence.[15]

Such an approach to understanding the female victim of violence is fundamentally nothing more than a sophisticated form of blaming the victim in the guise of scientific theory. In order to understand better why women are beaten, we need to stop asking inherently sexist questions (however professionally orthodox they may seem) about the woman and redirect our focus to the batterer and the situations in which these families find themselves.

The weakness of the generational transfer hypothesis for understanding these women's current problems can be seen in another issue: alcohol problems on the part of parents. Compare the low rates of alcohol and drug problems among these shelter residents (4 percent and 3 percent, respectively). If generational transfer of such problems existed, these residents should resemble their parents more. In fact, given the prevalence of both drugs and alcohol in American society, it is remarkable that these women's alcohol and drug problems are not more prevalent, regardless of the previous generation.

Thus the problems of one generation are not automatically visited on its children, however such a pattern would simplify things if it were true. In the 542 cases in this study, the relative absence of domestic violence in their childhood homes was not a safeguard against these women encountering violence in the homes they would establish.

WHY DO THEY STAY, AND WHAT MAKES THEM LEAVE?

Until recently, domestic violence was regarded as relatively rare and found nowhere but in the lowest classes of society. When it did surface, the question that most frequently occurred to people when they heard about a woman being battered was, "Why does she stay and take it?" The growing awareness that millions of American women are currently being abused, sometimes to the point of their lives being put in jeopardy, has begun to shift focus away from the question of why the woman endures beatings to a question more germane to uncovering the origins of such violence: "Why does he batter?"

Nevertheless, the first question is not irrelevant or totally misplaced. Examining some of the dimensions of why women stay in and later leave relationships with abusive men will help to develop insights into the plight of women who seek refuge in publicly supported shelters.

Staying

An important point to consider before all others deals with the frequency and duration of abuse that our 542 shelter residents experienced. In other words, how often were they beaten and how long did they tolerate it?

Most of these women had been battered more than once. A very few left after a single violent episode in their homes, but these were clearly exceptions. The majority of women had been beaten on the average anywhere from several times a month to daily, making violence part of their intimate relationships with men.

Just as important, only about one in ten women had experienced beatings for periods of less than six months. Most women had been living in a violent family environment for over a year. One in four lived in such a situation for *five years or more*. In two exceptional cases the women had been beaten for over 25 years. (See Table 2-5.)

When we looked at the frequency and duration of beatings in light of our Severity Index, an important finding emerged. *As the frequency of the battering episodes increased, the more severe they became.* Likewise, the longer that violence continued over months and years, the more serious and dangerous it became. In other words, over time the battering situations usually progressed from verbal abuse to punching the women often to using weapons. Moreover, such violence began to occur more frequently. Several women told us that they were somehow able to stand back one day and review how the pattern of violence had been intensifying; they then suddenly felt more afraid than at any time during a single beating.

WHY THEY FOUGHT

What did they argue about that ignited the violence? The women were asked what relevant issues had been associated with the beatings they received. The answers reveal a great deal about the pressures that weigh on young families and help provoke violence. (See Table 2-6.)

In a society where three fourths of males drink and where unknown but probably high percentages use drugs recreationally, it is not surprising that alcohol or drug use is connected to domestic violence in the majority of cases. From Hotline calls and the shelters' intake forms, we know that many of the batterers (in the women's estimations) had drug or alcohol problems and that many men were in fact intoxicated or high during violent episodes. Much of the violence occurred at the end of the day, in the late afternoon or early evening, when the man had had a few drinks "to unwind." But this does not mean that drugs or alcohol cause the violence; rather, it means that these substances can increase irritability, lower internal controls over temper and impatience, and lower inhibitions against being abusive. They act as catalysts, making violence more likely. In many cases they offer the batterer a handy, at-first-glance believable explanation for his violence (such as "I lost my head" or "I was so drunk I didn't know what I was doing"). The woman may also cling to this excuse when she tries to deny there is something fundamentally wrong in the relationship. Some women seemed to be trying to reassure themselves as much as convince us when they repeated that "He really isn't a bad father (husband/provider/mate) when he's sober."

That blaming violence on drugs and alcohol is actually nothing more than a rationalization is shown by the response, now a cliché, of one therapist to a batterer who relied on this excuse: "If you didn't know what you were doing, then why didn't you kill her?" In other words, it is no coincidence that violence stops short of homicide so often, even when batterers have supposedly "gone berserk" or been so drunk they did not know what they were doing. Too many women are choked to the brink of unconsciousness or death and then suddenly released, for booze or dope to be more than scapegoats for violence.[16]

Sex demands made by the batterers were one of the issues one fourth of the women mentioned. Given what we know already about the part that sexual domination often plays in the abusive relationship, this is not surprising. Nor is the fact that two thirds of the women mentioned the batterer's jealousy as a frequent issue. Batterers in this study and in others often seem to have an obsession with possessing the woman and managing her life down to incredibly small details. This possession mania often went (from an outsider's perspective) to absurd lengths. One shelter resident in Austin recalled:

> He treated me like a captive doll. He was obsessed with what I looked like (even though he gave me hell if I bought clothes without his permission). He'd say, "Let's go out for a drive in the country" or "Let's go to a mall." And then he'd pick the dress I had to wear, the shoes, even my slip and underwear. When I did pick out what I would wear on my own and *he* didn't approve . . . oh! Would he get steamed! It was like I was his little girl, unable to make my own decisions.

This possessiveness included not only the woman's clothes and appearance but also her time. Women in our study reported a frequent pattern: the man would make her account for virtually every waking minute. If she worked, he would time her on her way home from the job and call her daily during her lunch break. He would allot her so many minutes or hours for trips to stores, visits to friends, or other errands. He monitored her more closely than any nervous father ever did his adolescent daughter on her first date. Recalled one woman:

> He figured out it took 30 minutes exactly for me to get from work back home. I could never go out for a drink with the

> other women in the office. I could barely chat on the way
> out to the parking lot. God help me if there was a traffic
> jam or if a train came across town and blocked the road.
> He'd be pacing in the driveway, tapping his watch, ready
> to accuse me of having an affair after work.

Batterers also seemed preoccupied with the suspicion that at the first chance the women would cheat on them, engaging in affairs with other men. Such accusations often preceded a beating or contributed to the women's imprisonment. For example, Hilberman and Munson found strong evidence of what they termed "morbid jealousy" in almost all the cases they studied:

> Leaving the house for any reason invariably resulted in ac-
> cusations of infidelity which culminated in assault. Clinic
> visits were often made in secrecy, with some women regu-
> larly beaten when they returned from the clinic. Other
> channels of communications were also prevented. Friend-
> ships with women were discouraged, either by embarrassing
> the wife in front of her friends or by accusing her friends
> of being lesbians or "trash," with entry to the home denied.
> Many husbands refused to allow their wives to work. When
> the women did work, efforts were made to ensure that both
> spouses worked at the same place so that activities and
> friends could be monitored.[17]

We do not think the batterer uses the woman's alleged unfaithfulness merely as a convenient excuse to abuse her. There is good reason to think he actually believes it. The theme of jealousy, tied to sexual domination, appears so often in clinical psychological studies, in conversations with therapists who deal directly with battered women, and in the testimonies of the women themselves, it suggests the man is consumed with fears of the woman's promiscuity yet preoccupied with his own barely restrained sex drives. He projects this conflict onto the woman, becoming obsessed with preventing her (imagined) attempts to be adulterous. This is seen most clearly when we examine the issues surrounding the battering incident against the severity of the violence. Our Severity Index shows that violence resulting from highly emotional sex-related issues was much more severe than when the conflict concerns job or economic pressures or drinking behavior.

The last major issue which women reported being involved with abuse was job or financial pressure. Remember that the majority of these women had children and did not work outside the home. Thus, the man's income was critical to the family, and not unexpectedly (as in many families that are not violent) pressures at the job followed him home. Unfortunately for the woman in the situation, this is a source of frustration for the man over which she has little or no control. Shelters in Texas are only a few years old, having come into existence during the recession of the late 1970s and early 1980s. Therefore, we cannot know if job and financial problems would become a less important issue in domestic violence if the economy dramatically improved. However, it must be remembered that during this recession the "Sunbelt" region, of which Texas is a major part, has been affected less by economic problems than any other part of the United States. Indeed, Texas experienced economic growth and prosperity during 1980–82. Perhaps in a single-income household such as that of most of these women it is inevitable that outside financial pressures will always be an issue around which a batterer can focus his anger.

Finally, to understand a woman staying on in an abusive relationship it is important to know the man's reaction after he is violent toward the woman. After all, how he views his own violence is an important factor in the woman's hopes that the abuse will end. Elements discouraging the woman from leaving would be heartfelt apologies, promises never to be violent again, and so forth. Lenore Walker, in her book *The Battered Woman,* described a three-stage cycle of battering that includes a period of building tension, the battering episode itself, and then a "honeymoon" phase. During the honeymoon phase the man tries to make up with the woman, showers her with affection, and acts repentant (and may sincerely feel that way). One woman we interviewed outside the shelter sample told how her husband would take her and her daughter on trips, buy them both new clothes, return to the romantic style of their courtship, and in general help her erase memories of the episodes when he would literally wreck their furniture, throw china and glassware about the house, and abuse her both verbally and physically. He was a textbook case in terms of Walker's model, at least until his escalating violence, alcoholism, and adultery drove his wife out. Working irregular hours, he would abruptly return home and fly into a rage if his favorite meal was not on that evening's menu. Or he might request one dish for supper as he left for work and change his mind during the day, unknown to his wife. We asked her what he would say to justify his anger. She replied:

> He would call me all sorts of terrible names: a bitch, a cunt, a whore. He said I was a bad wife and ugly, that nobody else would want to eat my goddamned food. He'd make me feel like the lowest piece of shit on earth.

The vivid contrast between this mood and his "honeymoon" behavior made her understandably ambivalent about her marriage, for when it was good it was, by her own admission, very good. When it was bad, her life was literally in danger.

How prevalent was this sort of hot and cold relationship? In Chapter four we will examine in detail the usual feelings of batterers after they have abused their wives or girlfriends. However, we can say here that while some men do follow the three-stage cycle of battering that Lenore Walker describes, many do not. An alarming statistic from our study shows that half the men felt they were perfectly justified in striking women during family arguments. For them it was part of "maintaining discipline." Thus some women are kept in the relationship by ambivalent feelings. He does seem to be sorry. He does try to make amends. But other women know a different type of batterer, one who feels either that she deserves to be beaten or that he has the right as a male to hit her when they argue. Staying on in an abusive relationship for these women is better explained by their lack of resources and alternatives than by anything the man does to soothe her feelings (and bruises) after the violence.

Leaving

There are many pressures pushing a woman out of her home, yet others simultaneously holding her there. On one hand, there is continued physical abuse, much of it severe, and the knowledge that the husband or boyfriend does not consider his use of violence a problem, or that even if he does, he will use it again. On the other hand, there is the woman's lack of financial resources, often her responsibility for children, her lack of transportation, and the ambivalence caused by the man's alternating affection and abuse. Our final focus in this chapter deals with how and why the women left.

Much of the clinical psychological writings maintain that women rarely are able to leave an abusive situation voluntarily because they have been brutalized into a lethargic, submissive state of "learned helplessness." Lenore Walker coined this term to refer to the passive state of battered women who, after learning to anticipate violent attacks but being unable to do anything to prevent them, become like animals in experiments that are continually given electric shocks. Trapped in their cages and aware that no response can influence what happens to them, they become passive, submissive, and develop nervous disorders. (Learned helplessness is akin to the rape trauma syndrome, which can cause intense terror in women who have been sexually assaulted.[18]) Women in continually violent situations eventually lose their initiative to leave the situation, according to Walker:

> Repeated batterings, like electrical shocks, diminish the woman's motivation to respond. She becomes passive. Secondly, her cognitive ability to perceive success is changed. She does not believe her response will result in a favorable outcome, whether or not it might. Next, having generalized her helplessness, the battered woman does not believe any-

thing she does will alter any outcome, not just the specific situation that has occurred.[19]

The result, Walker maintains, is analogous to the state of experimental animals that had to be dragged from their cages after being shocked into inaction—they would not flee even when the doors were opened. Battered women, likewise, supposedly cannot leave the violent situation of their own volition.

Yet throughout our research we came to see that learned helplessness does not describe the courage and resourcefulness of the women we met. After all, these women did take the initiative and made the decision to leave their homes. This was never done without great sacrifice, and often risk, to each woman. Often their journey to the shelter was a calculated, narrowly timed escape that involved the nerve and planning of a prison break-out. They had to overcome the problems of excessively jealous husbands and having few funds. If caught by the batterer, in many cases they would face worse beatings. Often they had to leave with only the clothes they and their children were wearing and little more than loose change in their pockets, perhaps without necessary medication, and uncertain of what sort of place they were going to. However ambivalent, upset, and confused they were when they came to live communally in a shelter environment, they had retained their free will, their ability to make decisions and seek help. They had measured the costs of leaving a violent home against the price of staying and decided in favor of the former. In the jargon of shelter staffs, such women were "ready to leave." That is, it was their decision and not someone else's. They were and are survivors of domestic violence, not casualties; anything but passive as they actively sought some relief from intimate relations turned sour.

One suggestive study, done independently of ours, of the level of self-esteem of Dallas–Fort Worth women who enter shelters supports this position. In February 1982, forty women who entered the four shelters in the area were tested with a standardized index of self-esteem by Barbara Brown and Gina Brazzle, from the Graduate School of Social Work at the University of Texas at Arlington. Despite widespread assumptions and impressions that all women who seek shelter from battering must perforce have severely damaged egos as well as bodies, close to half (42 percent) of the women registered high in self-esteem when they entered the shelters. The authors concluded, ". . . women presenting themselves to a shelter cannot be assumed to suffer from low self-esteem." [20]

This finding agrees with that of Bruce J. Rounsaville on the passivity of the 31 battered women in his study: "The women in the sample were, in fact, not passive and isolated from others in that all had communicated with others about their abuse and had sought help." [21]

The role of shelters in helping such women is critical, for as we have seen, many have virtually nowhere or no one else to turn to for help. Once such shelters are established and word spreads through former residents, referrals by other social agencies, and the media, they fill up on a continual basis. The long waiting lists in Texas shelters (there are over 100 women as of this writing waiting to enter at Dallas's Family Place) are testimony to the overwhelming demand by women for safe places to escape domestic violence.

We can illustrate this demand. Women in our study were asked when they arrived at the shelters why they had remained in the violent situation, if they had not left immediately after a first incident. *Only 15 percent reported that they stayed out of affection for the man.* (See Table 2-7.) If we combine affection for the batterer with the expectation of women that they could save the marriage or relationship, we find that about four out of ten women remained because they still felt optimistic about the future of the relationship despite certain misgivings. But the majority stayed on for what we can call negative reasons: economic dependency, children (a reason related to economic dependency), direct coercion, and other reasons including indirect coercion such as threats related to leaving, threats to children, or the man threatening to commit suicide. The majority of women stayed, in other words, for lack of other feasible options.

A number of women explained to us what it was like to stay on in the home once there was no longer any affection left for the man. Debbie, a young housewife with a little girl, recalled:

> The saddest part towards the last year was actually the times between the beatings. When he wasn't there, the house was quiet, and believe it or not I was glad he was out, but lonely, too. When he was there and nonviolent, things were pretty cold between us. We wouldn't touch each other for months. After his drinking got worse the sex was pretty much his idea. By the end I felt my skin crawl when he'd start suggesting we go to bed. I was counting the days until I could leave, but it made the relationship so empty.

Shelters, once established, provide an option. Social workers Brown and Brazzle offer a similar conclusion for why women do not leave abusive relationships sooner. It is not nearly as often because of low self-esteem, learned helplessness, or other psychological reasons as is thought. Rather, they conclude that "economic restraints and fear that spouses would seek them out and do harm to their children or themselves if they left, have kept women in their homes, tolerating the beatings." [22]

Our final grim example illustrates the truth of their analysis. We use no pseudonyms because the event was reported in the media, and because the woman concerned is now dead. On September 13, 1982, the *Dallas Morning News* carried the headline: SHELTER FORCED TO TURN AWAY MANY ABUSE VICTIMS. The article read:

> Virtue Lynn Perry couldn't get the help she needed and wound up shot to death . . . She was desperate for a safe place to hide while trying to split up with her husband. The Family Center [sic], with a waiting list numbering in the hundreds, didn't have room for Mrs. Perry, however. Like four

out of five women who apply to the center, she was added to the waiting list. That was May 27. On Saturday, June 5, her husband traced her to the apartment of a female friend ... He stood at the bottom of the stairs, yelling, and would not go away, police reports said.

She agreed to go downstairs and talk to him. The confrontration ended, after five or six gunshots, with the death of Mrs. Perry, witnesses told police ...

When Family Place follow-up workers called to advise Mrs. Perry of her status on the waiting list ... they were shocked to learn she had been killed. But they've been shocked before—many, many times. "Many of the women who come here have suffered really severe, repeated physical abuse," [the executive director told the reporter] ... Demand on the center is increasing, she said.

THE PREDICAMENT OF THE BATTERED WOMAN

There are abused women who eventually sought assistance from places designed to give them safe haven from violent men. We have no reason to think these women are typical of all abused women. But they undoubtedly represent the more severe cases, who manage to find out about women's shelters and escape to them in lieu of having other resources to cope with their problem. (At a public hearing in Texas one of us used the word "flee" in testimony, and a feminist speaker later objected to that word as if we meant some cowardly act by the woman leaving a violent home. Far from it, these women frequently displayed great courage in leaving their abusive spouses and boyfriends and rescuing their children. Words like flight, escape, and so forth do not demean their actions.)

The predicament of women involved in family violence is a mosaic constructed out of numerous individual pieces. Among these pieces we can identify several critical ones:

First, there is the sustained violence that these women have faced. In terms of muscular strength and size, they are clearly the weaker sex, and because of it they have often suffered terrible physical injuries inflicted by much stronger men. Many of the batterers have deliberately taken advantage of uniquely female vulnerabilities, such as by beating the abdomen and breasts of pregnant women. Few of these women were battered only once. For most the violence occurred frequently, and escalated over a considerable period of time. We know from the telephone calls to shelters and from the waiting lists of women begging to find sanctuary in such places that the 542 shelter residents we studied are only the tip of the domestic violence iceberg in one metropolitan area of the country. Imagine how great the problem must really be among the four and a half million of the Dallas–Fort Worth area, and then imagine what it must be nationwide. Woman-battering is not some faddish social problem concocted by bleeding-heart social scientists or feminist writers. It is not going to go away, especially in light of the ever-increasing strains attacking the family in modern society.

Second, the economic vulnerability of the women who must depend on publicly supported shelters for safety is glaringly apparent. Usually these women have not tried to divide their time between home and a job. That is precisely what puts them at such a disadvantage once they have decided that they cannot change the man or stop the battering. They have few economic resources. They also have poor backgrounds for ever earning such resources. These women have the primary responsibility for their children (who are most often very young).

These facts make simply packing up and leaving a violent home a gigantic act of resolve and a tremendous risk for the individual woman. She risks further angering a violent man who may punish her, losing her sole means of financial support, and facing the recriminations ("Why weren't you a better wife?") of friends and relatives. Rather than asking "Why doesn't she leave," given the large number of obstacles confronting such a woman, a better question would be "How can she leave?" The availability of a safe shelter that recognizes her problems and needs is one such answer that we have found. One sociologist summarized the predicament:

> The fewer alternatives a woman has to her marriage, the fewer resources she possesses in terms of formal education or job skills, the more "entrapped" she is in her marriage and the less likely she is to seek help or get a divorce after being beaten by her husband.[23]

Third, there is lack of evidence for blaming the victim. Most of these women did not subtly invite violence by having been raised in violent homes and conditioned to expect it, *because they were not raised that way.* They are not masochists. There is little evidence, in other words, that the women who enter shelters were conditioned to involve themselves with violent men or suffer violence passively. They find themselves caught in the situation after marriage, more an accident of bad luck than a predictable outcome based on their socialization. The rapidly growing demand for space in shelters testifies to the willingness of women, despite the costs, to leave bad situations given a chance.

A final word on the women. We said before that the women who make their way to shelters are survivors, not casualties, of domestic violence. The casualties are the unfortunate women who never leave abusive relationships, some fated to die or deteriorate in health to the point of death or mental stupor, others to live in a state of semi-imprisonment or fear that saps their lives of much potential and vitality. Perhaps these are the victims of learned helplessness, or are devout followers of religious or sexist ideologies that make an idolatry of preserving the family unit regardless of its destructive outcomes for family members.

But the women in our study are true survivors, at least for now. Human relationships continue, evolve, or stagnate. Not all these women may survive one, two, or three years from this writing. Indeed, we know from follow-up studies that some have not survived leaving the shelters. They committed suicide, were committed to mental hospitals, or were killed. Once women leave shelters they have possibilities before them, but no certainties. Survival for these women is not necessarily a foreseeable goal but it represents a possible option that they at least chose the first time they came to a shelter, but which they have to work out further when they move on.

3

CHILDREN: THE MOST
HELPLESS VICTIMS

Excluding professionals working daily with child abuse cases, no one we talked to during our research reacted dispassionately to the problem. Indeed, it aroused extraordinary, vindictive anger in otherwise respectable citizens whose backgrounds ranged across a broad spectrum, such as schoolteachers, police officers, college presidents, ministers, university students, auto mechanics, and landlords. This anger was vehement and unrelenting. Many acquaintances and colleagues suggested without so much as batting an eye that child abusers deserved castration, execution, or worse. These abusers were even condemned as subhumans. In short, no one seemed able to separate personal emotional outrage from objective attempts to understand the phenomenon.

Yet there is an irony here. While the concept *child abuse* and its companion concept *child neglect* have numerous official definitions, the actual lines that separate them from ordinary parental discipline or care are not clearly drawn. We defined the terms formally in Chapter one, but here we want to begin by noting the ambiguity of such distinctions. Consider the following example, which illustrates the difficulty of separating discipline and abuse:

> Mrs. C. is a middle-class homemaker with three children. She discovers that her youngest son, John, is afraid of vacuum cleaners. When he misbehaves during her housework, Mrs. C. moves the roaring machine closer to him and (from her perspective) jokingly threatens to suck him up into the hose. However, John has seen the vacuum cleaner make things disappear. He is *really* afraid that this will happen to him. (Like all children, he thinks in terms of concrete events, not abstractions.) So he backs away in fear and obeys her.

Is this child abuse? Middle-class parents educated in modern principles and techniques of child psychology might disapprove of such "discipline" as psychological abuse. Other less enlightened parents might consider it relatively harmless. (And it may keep John in line.)

But suppose John takes Mrs. C.'s threats for granted, so that she has to move toward John as if to really suck him into the vacuum hose. One day he becomes terrified by this and bursts out of the house into the street, directly in front of a speeding automobile. John is hit by the car, suffering a number of internal injuries and broken bones. Is *this* child abuse?

The staffs of women's shelters across the nation continually face similar problems of identifying child abuse and neglect. Though such places were originally formed in response to the abuse of women, the fact that children are usually involved, sometimes also as victims, soon became inescapable. Family violence touches children in various ways even if it is never directly aimed at them, and as we shall see, sorting out its effects sometimes requires subtle and patient detective work. In this chapter we look at the 803 children that 424 of our study's 542 battered women brought with them into the shelters. The questions we want to ask concern their involvement in family violence: How often is the abusing man's anger turned on children in the family? What are its effects on the children? What does such abuse say about the American family as an institution?

These questions will help us to scrutinize one of the saddest aspects of family violence. The victimization of children is surely the ultimate betrayal of what a family is universally supposed to be: a warm, receptive, nurturing haven from an often cruel world. Child abuse is literally a perversion of the archetypal bond of human intimacy, that of parent and child. Yet by studying such cases we can better understand the dynamics of family violence and paradoxically learn more about the American family in general.

THE DIRECT EFFECTS OF CHILD ABUSE

During a two-year period, 424 shelter residents in our study who fled their homes took their children with them. Another 28 battered mothers had managed to leave their children with relatives or friends before arriving at shelters in Dallas and Denton, Texas. Based on these facts, we conclude that the average battered woman brings two young children with her; many enter with more. The average age of the children in our study was five and a half; over half the youngsters were preschoolers. One child in five was an infant (less than one year old). At any given time there were at least twice as many children in a shelter as there were battered women. This fact is important because it shows the great pressures on staffs of shelters to recognize and deal with the children as victims of family violence.

After a woman had been admitted to a shelter, she was interviewed by a staff member and asked, among other things, about violence directed toward her children. The questions were quite specific and dealt with each child. The women's answers reveal how often children became the victims of family violence. *Almost half* (45 percent) of the children had been physically abused or seriously neglected, often both. This is a rate

1500 percent higher than national averages for families in the general population!

The ways they were abused resemble how their mothers had been beaten. Apart from being verbally abused, the children had been punched, slapped, and kicked. A few had been cut or burned noticeably. Fifty-five of the children had been beaten in a variety of other ways, such as by men using trouser belts and belt buckles. One of the most "popular" weapons used to whip children in the Dallas–Fort Worth Metroplex was an extension cord. Other children, particularly smaller ones, were abused in ways overlapping with neglect. For example, painful confinement, or "hog-tying," was common. (See Table 3-3.) Reported one Dallas shelter worker:

> We had a kid whose father was alcoholic. He used to leave at night to go out to the bars. Before he left he would tie the child in the playpen and turn the TV on and then go out for hours. The kid had binding marks around the feet and up the legs even to the groin.

A small toddler left alone strapped to the rungs of a playpen, eventually soiling his diapers, without anyone to respond to his cries of discomfort, is a disturbing picture in most people's minds. Even worse were the cases of sexual violence, or incest, committed by either of the parents on both little boys and girls. There were twelve children identified by these preliminary interviews who had been sexually abused by their parents, usually their fathers or stepfathers. This abuse ranged from fondling and stroking the child's genitals to inducing the child to have oral intercourse to actual rape, or penetration. The abuse most often occurred in a pseudo-instructional situation prefaced by a statement such as "Tonight we're going to learn about sex." These instances presented the most horrifying examples of abuse that we encountered.

Sometimes they were intertwined with abuse of the mother, as in the case of one stepfather who ordered his eight- and nine-year-old stepdaughters to watch as he forced his pregnant wife down on the kitchen floor and inserted a broom handle into her vagina. He next penetrated the nine-year-old girl with the broom, forcing the eight-year-old sister and her mother to watch.

Sometimes the sexual abuse was more subtle. Recalled a shelter coordinator:

> I think one of the cases about sex abuse that particularly sticks out in my mind and is still very upsetting to me concerned a family where the oldest girl, a fifteen-year-old, was being sexually abused by the stepfather. This man took care of a home for retired gentlemen. She was not only forced to have relationships with the father but also he set her up for relations with other residents, even with the handymen who worked around the home. The fifteen-year-old saw herself as protecting the others [her siblings] by having sex with the stepfather, so that he wouldn't touch them. But the children would end up telling Mom, and Mom's response was to get very angry toward them and then turn suicidal. She would go to bed for days on end. The children then felt extremely angry toward her for not doing anything. This fellow also made the fifteen-year-old and her sisters watch as he had sex with their mother. It seemed so prostituting of that girl. She saw herself as trying to protect the others by having sex with the stepfather, yet she felt conflict and guilt because she had failed. It obviously affected those girls. They're all in residential [psychiatric] treatment now.

Many times the marks of violence on children were obvious. The most common signs were bruises and cuts or lumps on heads. Occasionally bandages and casts revealed burns and broken bones. (See Table 3-4.) The link to woman-battering also seems obvious when we examine child abuse in light of our Severity Index: *Men who battered women more severely were also likely to harm their children.*

But not all injuries were immediately visible, and the women did not always admit to child abuse during the first interview. Sometimes the staff members' discoveries of such abuse were pure chance. Recalled one worker:

I remember one child in particular afraid of scalding water. Chris was a four-year-old boy who eventually was taken out of the shelter to go live with his grandparents while his mother continued to stay here. His abuse wasn't something she could or would easily admit to. There weren't any marks on him when he entered. But every time someone turned on a shower he'd go berserk. He was generally afraid of water, but the shower made him go crazy. The hysterics alerted us to something there. Finally, between Chris and talking to and questioning the mother, we learned the problem. Her husband would discipline Chris . . . he would turn the shower on until the water got real hot and then stick the kid under the shower. So when the kid heard the shower turned on in the shelter he went into hysterics.

Sometimes play therapy sessions with smaller children like Chris would allow them to reveal violence in the family in ways that they were otherwise too young to describe. In the case of Chris, the shelter therapists allowed him to put sexless wood figures into toy cars and act out his mother and father driving. Chris always had the father's car drive recklessly and destructively, crashing into his mother's car. Significantly, he invariably ended each wild drive with his father going over a "cliff" and dying, then being "reborn" to repeat the scenario again and again.

Such play strategies, which psychologists refer to as *projective techniques,* are often used to discover unreported abuse and to gauge the severity of emotional damage to the children. The principle behind these techniques can also be used to disclose sexual abuse that young children have obvious difficulty describing. The use of father, mother, and child dolls to give preschool children an opportunity to act out how they were abused began with two Oregon women, Brenda Watson and Roi Hokinson, who worked with young rape victims. Rather than use anatomically correct models (which were unavailable), they put together their own rag dolls and reconstructed the abuse from the scenarios worked out by the children. This is now a strategy being widely used, even by police. For example, the Dallas Police Department investigates about 200 child-abuse cases each month, and about 100 of them are sex-abuse cases. During our research we read the following in the *Dallas Morning News*:

> Earlier this year, a Dallas baby sitter suspected that one of her charges, a two-year-old girl, was being sexually abused by her mother and the mother's boyfriend. The baby sitter called child welfare workers, who in turn contacted the police. But officers were unable to get any details from the child. She was just too young to talk about what happened to her.
>
> "She could only grab herself between the legs and say, 'Mommy hurt,'" says Grady Ford, an investigator with the Dallas Police Department.
>
> Without specific testimony from the child, police could not pursue their investigation. So they presented the little girl with a set of "show and tell" dolls and asked her to demonstrate, with the dolls, what had been done to her. By using the rag dolls . . . the girl was able to show police how she had been sexually abused by the mother and boyfriend.[1]

There are many reasons that women might want to hide the fact that their children are abused. Some women fear that if the abuse is discovered their children will be automatically taken away by the authorities, regardless of who really did the abusing. Other women may themselves be the child abusers and fear reprisals. Some women may be uncertain about returning home to their husbands. Their reluctance to report child abuse becomes a way of protecting the male abuser; otherwise they face the prospect of turning the man in and burning the bridges back to their marriages forever. Still other women are ashamed. Acknowledging the child abuse reveals their failure to care for their children, so they say nothing.

For whatever reason, many forms of child abuse go unreported or are covered up during the first wave of interviews with newly admitted shelter residents. Sometimes the woman has been so inured to violence, perhaps since her own childhood, that she does not recognize all but the most flagrant abuse as a problem. We have good reason to suspect, there-fore, that our initial finding that 45 percent of the children have been abused or seriously neglected is actually an under-estimate. Professional staff members pick up the more subtle signs of harm to children after a woman and her children have lived in the close quarters of a shelter over a period of weeks. For example, Family Place in Dallas, which collects detailed child abuse statistics for a nationally funded special project on children, noted that during the first quarter of 1982 half the children had been physically abused, over one in three had been neglected, almost one in ten had been sexually abused, one in five had been mistreated in more than one way, and one in four was seriously emotionally disturbed as a result of fam-ily violence.[2] Thus, the first interview only picks up the grossest and most serious physical abuse; more thorough observation over time reveals additional evidence of children's victimiza-tion.

The direct physical effects of child abuse are prevalent and observable. But they are only the most obvious results of fam-ily violence and perhaps, in the long run, the least important. To gain a fuller understanding of the harm family violence does to children, we need to take a look at its indirect effects as well.

NEGLECT AND THE INDIRECT EFFECTS OF ABUSE

Living in a violent home took its toll on the children we studied just as it did on their mothers, for abuse was seldom a one-time occurrence. For the majority of the children, adult violence aimed at them was a weekly or even daily fact of life. (See Table 3-6.) Even though many were still in their pre-school years, two out of three children had been abused for at least one year. Some of the older ones had been abused for as long as seven years or more. (See Table 3-5.) And although not all children were direct victims of family violence, only the very smallest were unaware of it. Nine out of ten mothers reported that their children had seen the fathers, husbands, or boyfriends beating them. (See Table 3-2.)

The emotional trauma and disruption of anything resembling a normal family routine produced by this violence could be seen both in the children and in how their mothers managed them in the shelters. This less immediate kind of harm can be thought of as either neglect or indirect, emotional "fallout" from physical abuse.

Neglect

> Keeping your ass together and trying to run a household wasn't easy. It all finally fell apart. That's why I left. He was using just anything to blame me for, then he'd get rough with me. He'd smash up furniture and then say the house was a mess. He'd never come home at the same time, but I was supposed to have dinner—and not just *any* dinner—ready whenever. [He'd say] I never liked sex enough, I never dressed as well as he wanted. Once he gave me a bloody nose, then became angrier that I couldn't go out to a show with him because it hadn't stopped bleeding. I know it was rough on my two kids... irregular meals, all the noise, the house sometimes *was* a complete mess when I'd lay in bed with a headache from being hit...

Shortly before she left home with her children, this shelter resident became concerned that she was no longer an effective mother and homemaker. She saw the physical beatings her husband reserved for her alone nevertheless causing her to neglect her children. Some mornings she was too sore and bruised to do more than fix them breakfast. That was what finally convinced her to leave: the realization that her children were being harmed even though their father never hit them.

This pattern of actually forcing a woman into a situation where she neglects her children parallels other research showing the relation of alcohol abuse to neglect. Recall that according to many shelter residents, their husbands and boyfriends had been drinking heavily or taking drugs close to the times of being violent. In the opinions of these women many of the men had serious alcohol or drug-abuse problems. Val D. MacMurray, at the University of Calgary in Alberta, Canada, summarized how alcoholism contributes to child neglect:

> . . . neglect is the most common form of abuse suffered by children of alcoholics . . . many of the alcoholic fathers avoided the possibility of abuse by making a conscious decision to refrain from disciplining their children while drinking. *The wives, rather than the children, became the victims of physical outbursts, while the children were more likely to suffer emotional neglect from both or either parent.*[3] (Italics ours.)

Neglect of children, of course, can be something that occurs in homes where there is no violence. It is likely that a number of battered women would have neglected their children if they had not been abused. For example, one woman who entered one of the shelters we studied came with two small children, one eighteen months old, the other a three-month-old infant. At first, after seeing her limited skills as a parent, shelter staff suspected she was mentally retarded. However, tests showed she was not. The staff tried counseling her, but it changed nothing. She was an inept, as well as an uninterested, mother. As the shelter coordinator concluded, "We realized there was no motivation on her part." Other residents complained of the two children crying constantly and being left unattended, their dirty diapers thrown on the floor of the room and ignored by the mother. They complained of the smell. The diaper stench alone drove the staff to do something about the mother's lack of interest in looking after her children. Recalled one staff member:

> We'd go back into her room, the dirty diapers there from the night before, and tried to work with her. The baby would constantly be prop-fed, her head propped up with dirty, wet soiled diapers, the bottle stuck in her face.

Finally Child Protective Services were called, but before they could intervene the woman literally went out the back door one night, taking the two small children with her. Two months later word came back to the shelter that the youngest child had died soon after.

No one is officially certified for parenting, so unfortunate as it may be for many innocent, unlucky children, the odds are that such incompetent, ill-suited, disinterested mothers will be among women seeking shelter safety from abusive men. However, more important are the mothers as in our first example, who are virtually forced into neglecting their children by men who demand full-time attention themselves or who numb the women with serious violence so greatly that their care of other family members suffers. Theirs are the more typical stories of child neglect, a neglect that is more often the result of a woman trying to conserve her energy to protect or heal herself physically than a conscious lack of interest in her offspring.

Many women find that shelters provide the first opportunity in a long time that they and their children can enjoy simple pleasures, such as eating meals in peace on a regular schedule. The mother does not have to push her children into a back bedroom while her husband is on the rampage. She can once again give attention to the concerns and joys of following the daily adventures of young children, reading to them before bedtime because it is mutually pleasurable, not simply to "act busy" or escape from the man's anger. Children's schoolwork, their clothes, their comments about the world at large can once again reassert themselves when their mothers' fears of violence or even day-to-day survival diminish.

The Indirect Effects of Abuse

Children who have been abused or who have witnessed their parents violently fighting communicate the stress they feel in many ways. Some show signs of what psychologists call "regres-

sive behavior," reverting back to habits of very young childhood: thumb-sucking, bed-wetting, or infantile temper-
tantrums. These children are trying to find peace of mind by
escaping to earlier, safer times when they did not have to worry
about violence or were unaware of it. In extreme cases, such a
way of coping with inescapable strain and pressure could result
in schizophrenia or other serious emotional problems.

Many children in shelters also "act up," particularly when
they first arrive. They may seem extremely aggressive, noisy,
and rowdy, fighting with each other or energetically finding
ways to be disruptive. This is, of course, their way of handling
the strains of moving to a new environment where they must
live with several dozen people, without their own toys or other
possessions. They often are old enough to know that something
major has happened between their parents. Since a particularly
violent argument often precedes a woman leaving her home,
and her departure may have been dramatic and abrupt, there
is a feeling of tension in the mother, which the child can sense.
And paradoxically, even if they were abused themselves by their
father, children may still love him. They often ask their mothers and shelter staff workers when will they see Dad, will he be
coming to visit them, and so forth. Like their mothers, they
are unsure what the implications of coming to the shelter are
for the family's future.

But there are instances that show a more serious, long-lasting
kind of effect of living in a violent home. These can also be
considered child abuse, even when the children are not directly
injured, because their emotional health is damaged. The young
person's basic need and tendency to love and identify with a
parent, particularly for boys and their fathers, becomes warped
into an imitation of violence that bodes ill for the future. In
studying thousands of calls to the Hotline at Dallas's Family
Place we discovered various cases where an adolescent or
younger son actually participated in his father's abuse of his
mother. One woman told in tears how the father would per-
suade the boy to hold his mother's legs while the man sat on her

chest and beat her face and head with his fists. In another instance the father would chase his wife around the house, throwing objects at her, and the six-year-old son would gleefully
follow after, hurling his own toys, mimicking his father's shouts
and curses, as if it was all a game.

A more subtle effect of watching parental violence showed up
in a shelter resident's nine-year-old son, Markie. From time to
time Markie's father argued terribly with his mother, always
ending with the threat to commit suicide. On occasion the
father would take a loaded pistol and storm into the bedroom,
lock the door, and fire the gun into the wall, screaming as if
in pain. The frantic mother, beating on the door in near hys-
teria, was precisely the result he wanted. Markie took all this
in, and with the help of his younger sister began pulling off
similar mock suicides. Markie would get his sister to run to
their mother, shouting, "Come to Markie's room, he has a
rope around his neck and can't breathe!" The frightened
mother would find an immobile Markie with a window-blind
cord wrapped around his neck, lying on the floor or sprawled
on the bed. As she rushed to help him he would suddenly open
his eyes and grin, saying, "Hi, Mom!" Children naturally try
to have some control over their world, to cause things to happen, to make things work. Unfortunately, Markie had learned
too well from his violent father how psychological abuse could
affect his mother. So had his sister.

One final anecdote is in some ways mild, but it made us
think about the almost endless repercussions that family violence may have for children. Waiting to talk to a director in
one south Texas shelter on a Saturday morning, we could hear
children's boisterous voices in the dining room and hallways.
Suddenly a five-year-old girl in pigtails came streaking into the
front room where we sat, her freckle-faced ten-year-old brother
right behind her. She darted and swerved away, avoiding his
outstretched hands. She was shrieking in delight, he was laughing and panting. As he chased her down a hallway, he roared:
"I'm going to kill this bitch!"

Granted, we are middle-class university professors. It is understandable that we were shocked. Granted, too, children often say things, including profanity, to each other that they would never say in front of their parents. But here we have a simple yet telling example of what a violent parent obviously said in front of his kids. Perhaps in the long run these particular children will be none the worse for having been exposed to verbal and physical abuse in their home. Certainly the example of their mother leaving the violent home and taking them with her showed them clearly that violence is not wholesome or normal.

But in the short run they were certainly more desensitized to verbal abuse, a little more accepting of it than they would be otherwise. This is the most disturbing element running through even the relatively mild cases of family violence where children are not directly struck. There is an unknown after-effect from even being exposed to violence in the home. How long it continues to affect children undoubtedly differs from person to person and from family to family. But we know it does.

That is why the young son of a battered woman playfully chasing his little sister, calling her a bitch and threatening to kill her *in fun,* gives us pause.

CHILD ABUSE AND FAMILY VALUES

The irony of all family violence, but particularly of child abuse, is that it occurs on *safe ground.* The notion of safe ground, or safe territory, has been developed by an author studying rape of women on the worksite. Home and job settings are examples of safe ground, places where we normally expect to be surrounded by familiar faces, not strangers. They are places where we supposedly can be more at ease, less on the defensive, than we would be on city streets or in crowds.[4]

When crimes of violence occur on safe ground, we feel a

sense of anger and outrage. Things like that aren't supposed to happen there. This is undoubtedly one reason it is still a difficult task for social workers, psychologists, and sociologists to convince the general public (in addition to legislators, judges, juries, and district attorneys) that family violence is a major problem, not just some rare, freakish event. That the safe territory of the home is violated frequently by its *members,* not outsiders, disturbs many people. Unfortunately it disturbs them in the wrong way. It is a fact they would rather not confront. It is more comforting simply to shrug off woman-batterers and child abusers as perverts or psychotics or the families as bizarre. In writing about child abuse, sociologist Frank Weed made a similar observation:

> One of our ways of avoiding responsibility for the widespread cultural pattern of using violence and aggression against children is to see the abusive parent as mentally ill. In this way the phenomenon of child abuse is removed from the everyday "normal" patterns of child rearing and is foisted off on a small minority of "sick" parents.[5]

Rather than seeing the problem as one of character faults in the parents, Weed suggests that certain key values and beliefs in American culture, values and beliefs that we normally view as wholesome and beneficial, actually set up the possibility for child abuse to occur. In his opinion child abusers are not so radically different from other parents, however difficult that fact may be to accept.

> We must remember that the abnormal is as much a part of our culture as the normal aspects of life and that the abusive parent may be only an extreme example of the [same] cultural pattern that is going on in everyday life.[6]

Weed identifies three themes or cultural patterns in American society that make a certain amount of child abuse almost inevitable. First, Americans have traditionally prized *self-reliance*. Ministers, school teachers, and soap-box politicians have always preached the virtues of ambition and individual responsibility. But there is a hidden message in the value of being self-reliant, and that is control. It is good to control other people, particularly those people who may lay claims on you. Without such control real self-reliance is not possible. In the family it takes the form of a man being the head of the household. Even if he is not its only bread-winner, he makes the final decisions.

A second value pattern emphasizes not only respect for authority but also in many instances that authority's *right to use force* if necessary to maintain itself. In some other cultures a person in authority would be seen as weak or disgracing himself if he used force against a weaker person. But in American culture a parent does not lose face or suffer any loss of esteem for hitting a child unless the seriousness of the blow is totally out of line with the relative harmlessness of the child's offense. In fact, men and women may be seen as (and consider themselves) better parents if they do physically discipline their children than if they do not.

A third value pattern deals with *effectiveness* and *efficiency*. The concept of effectiveness involves getting things done, while the concept of efficiency means getting things done with a minimum of effort. This desire for efficiency and effectiveness in family relationships results in there being a limit to the amount of time and energy adults will put into reason and persuasion when they are trying to get children to do what they want them to do.

Put these three values together, and you have the ideal situation for potential child abuse. Forceful discipline is successful, at least in the short run, in getting a child to change his behavior (though not necessarily his attitude); it certainly can be less time-consuming and less trouble than trying to reason or debate with the child; it is justifiable because parents are authority figures with the right (and duty) to discipline; and such discipline gives the parent control.

What Weed argues, therefore, is that American culture structures the family so that some violent parents, low on child-rearing skills, can take advantage of the weakness and helplessness of children to use simple, uncomplicated force as an efficient way of maintaining order. Moreover, certain taken-for-granted American values tell them they are right in doing this.

This does not mean that Americans have a monopoly on child abuse, or that the three cultural values we have described cannot be found in other countries as well. Nor does it mean that emotional illness, such as sadism or sexual perversion, can be completely dismissed. Sociologist Richard Gelles, for example, has called for a more integrated explanation of what makes a child abuser, blending theories of psychological abnormality with what sociologists have found out about family strain and children's imitation of violent parents. However, simply assuming that all abusers are mentally ill because they offend our personal sensibilities about how children should be raised will help us little in understanding the roots of the problem.[7]

Weed's theory shows how mild or "normal" physical discipline (such as spanking) can escalate under all sorts of pressures and frustrations until a child is literally in danger, and yet the abuser will still feel the abuse is appropriate. Our family values assume good intentions on the part of parents, and abusers can always rationalize that what they are doing is in the best interests of the child. James I. McGovern, an investigator in the Illinois Department of Children and Family Services, found this pattern when trying to convince parents that they were in fact abusive:

A case in point is that of Denise, age six, who was beaten by her mother with a belt for not washing her clothes while staying temporarily with an aunt. The mother removed all of the girl's clothing and beat her in front of several other children and adults, gagging Denise with her own underpants to stifle her screams. Denise was placed in foster care immediately after being treated and released at a hospital, but a thorough investigation was then needed for court and planning purposes. Throughout the investigation and subsequent court hearings, the mother maintained a friendly and open attitude but never expressed remorse, either for the reported incident or for previous beatings that had left many scars on Denise's body. Instead she maintained that Denise needed to be beaten because other modes of discipline didn't work with her, that she continued to misbehave and do things that were dangerous. The mother couldn't understand that her beating the girl wasn't "working" either, that it was instead a great impediment to Denise's health and development. The mother had already been involved in several counseling programs prior to the reported beating, but her attitude toward Denise was apparently too deeply rooted to be influenced.[8]

It is easy to see how family violence involving children can become fairly serious before others become aware of it or before authorities are willing to do anything about it. We know that many cases fall into the gray area between normal discipline and abuse. And the expression "a man's home is his castle" is not an extinct attitude in the minds of many men. Also, to many people, what goes on inside the four walls of others' homes is considered their own business and nobody else's. The tragedy is that it becomes literally everybody's business (in the sense that public officials have to cope with it) only after a good deal of harm has been done. This is a clear example of how yet another time-honored American value—the sanctity of the home—promotes the possibility of violence. We are not arguing against civil liberties, rights of privacy, or parental control of children. We *are* arguing for a greater amount of healthy cynicism about the home. It has no special exemption from violence, and indeed when violence happens there it can go unnoticed and unchecked for a long time.

Thus the children in our study were not merely baggage

that women took with them when they left violent homes. The children too were frequently victims. This is a fact about shelters and the services they provide that many legislators, along with the public, do not fully realize. For this reason it would be best to reconsider how we usually refer to such havens: more than women's shelters, they are truly family shelters, serving a potential clientele staggering in size.

4
MEN: THE PERPETRATORS
OF VIOLENCE

Ingleborg Dedichen lived with the famous Greek shipping magnate Aristotle Onassis for over twelve years. In a magazine interview she described an incident in which Onassis beat her severely until he finally quit from exhaustion. The following day, instead of apologizing, Onassis explained, "All Greek husbands, I tell you, all Greek men without exception, beat their wives. It's good for them." And he laughed.[1]

Violence by men against women in American homes is usually not done with such cavalier smugness. The average man does not marry or begin a romance with a woman for the purpose of having someone around to beat whenever the mood comes over him. It is safe to say that in most cases men enter a relationship with the same romantic notions as women. Yet family violence experts such as Lenore Walker estimate that in almost half of American marriages the husband eventually becomes physically aggressive at least once, settling family disputes with his fists or worse. Sometimes things deteriorate to the point that the relationship between man and woman is little more than one of fear and outright cruelty. This grim fact seems to be true in all social classes, among all occupations, religious groups, and races, and at all ages. Whoever and wherever you are in American society, the odds are very good that someone you know fairly well—the man in your home, a friend, a next-door neighbor, a co-worker—batters some or all of the members of his family.

These batterers are a little-understood element of family violence. As far as scientific research is concerned, they are featureless men. Because it is the women who seek help from shelters, rarely the men, we usually get an unclear view of them as human beings, and that is secondhand. Generally researchers have not been able to learn if batterers, apart from their violent episodes, are otherwise decent citizens. Few concrete facts are known about their backgrounds or if these men were themselves victims of family violence when they were children. They emerge in the horror stories of family disputes as villains or monsters. As a result, a good deal of untested folklore has grown up around their alleged characteristics, as has evolved around the characteristics of the women victims.

Most experts in the field of family violence rarely consider the male abuser to be mentally ill or psychotic (although we may want to conclude that he is a sadist or pervert when we see the grossest examples of violence against helpless victims). Many believe it likely that the batterer was raised as a child in a violent home. Other experts suggest that the seriously violent batterer is a sociopath, a catch-all clinical term now popular among social scientists. Labeling him a sociopath means basically that the man has a stunted personality, that he lacks the full capacity to empathize or identify emotionally with other people. As a result, he is capable of committing acts that seem callous, brutal, or wanton. He lacks, by ordinary standards, a fully developed conscience and sense of morality.

It is tempting to play armchair psychiatrist and casually make sweeping generalizations about the psychological states of battering men. The extremes of violence they sometimes reach make it easy to assume that they are aberrant in some way.

However, in this chapter we will try, using facts rather than mere speculation, to dispel some of the confusion about extremely violent batterers. Each of the 542 women in our sample gave a great deal of background information on the man who beat her, and often her children, when she entered the shelter, including what she knew of his childhood experiences and his parents. We have tried to be cautious in using this kind of information. Fortunately, many women who did not know enough about the men's backgrounds to answer accurately said so when they were interviewed. This information thus presents us with the largest collection of batterers yet studied and therefore gives an excellent opportunity to learn more about these unknown, often ignored men. Our own observations and discussions with batterers and with their counselors will shed further light on the male side of family violence.

Here we will be asking a trio of important questions about these men:

First, *what kind of man is a violent batterer?* For example, is he a young man raised in a society that glorifies violence through its media or an older man with the more traditional beliefs that a woman's place is to accept physical discipline? Does his education, his job, or his race have anything to do with his violence? Is the batterer a generally violent person outside the home as well, or does he "get it off his chest" behind closed doors at home and then become a respectable citizen to the world at large?

Second, *was the batterer himself a victim of childhood family violence?* In Chapter two we found the generational transfer hypothesis to be of little value in helping us understand why women remained in violent relationships. There was no evidence that most of them had been raised to consider such abuse a normal part of a married woman's lot in life. Does this hypothesis have a better record when applied to the men? In other words, is he the "violent son of a violent son?" If so, what does such a finding suggest for helping these men?

Third, *what is the batterer's reaction after a violent episode?*

There is still a good deal of debate about what happens in the aftermath of violence. Some experts, and many of the women themselves, say he is repentant, kind, or loving at least for a while. Others bluntly observe, as did one shelter resident, "He still don't give a damn for what he done." The man's reaction can be an important indication of why so many marriages hang together as long as they do. It also can point to ways that these men might someday be changed into nonbatterers.

WHAT KIND OF A MAN
IS A VIOLENT BATTERER?

The Dallas–Fort Worth area batterers in our study had much in common with the women, described in Chapter two. For example, most were husbands rather than boyfriends. Most were only a few years older than their mates, in their late twenties or early thirties.

Background characteristics of the men point to some important types of stress that play a role in their violence. (See Table 4-1.) One such factor is education. A little more than half the batterers had graduated from high school, but few had gone to college. Almost half had never graduated from high school. (This does not mean that men with college degrees never batter their wives, only that women who are desperate enough to flee from severe violence to a publicly supported shelter often have been living with someone having a minimal formal education.) A low educational level does not cause violence, of course, but it aggravated the frustrations felt by both the men and women in our study when they quarrelled. Among other things, education can provide people with alternatives for resolving family disagreements. It makes it more likely that people will value nonviolent ways of settling arguments. Handling the many conflicts and differences of opinion that happen in any marriage or sexual relationship can be thought of as a problem requiring certain skills. Nonviolent skills include habits of negotiation, learning to give and take, and, just as important, being able, not only willing, to express honest feelings about an issue. Violence can be thought of as a tactic for a man to fall back on when he finds himself losing an argument or if he lacks negotiating skills altogether. It can certainly be less time-consuming. In other words, the relative lack of education of many of these men, similar to that of many of the women, means that when the inevitable problems of living together arose the two parties involved were often ill-equipped to sort things out peacefully.

Batterers in group therapy whom we met and listened to seemed aware (and frustrated to an extent) that they had difficulty arguing with women over even trivial issues without the argument quickly turning violent. Virtually all resembled our profile of a batterer with relatively little education. They laughed nervously as they told their individual stories and listened sympathetically to others, almost afraid of sharing their powerful feelings of affection and anger toward women even with other men in the same situation. For example, one young man we'll call Bob exemplified this lack. He told his story to a circle of seated men with his eyes moving rapidly back and forth across his hands in his lap, his face lowered toward the floor. Bob had married just out of high school. He was now working as well as attending university classes part-time. According to Bob, he would come home at the end of the day physically drained and almost immediately would lie down on the sofa to rest. His wife, who did not work or go to school, always had "a list of jobs for me to do" and would try to get Bob off the sofa with comments such as, "Well, are you going to lay around on your ass all day or do something useful?" Bob would reply with something equally unpleasant, and ineffective in terms of getting some sympathy for his fatigue. From there the exchange escalated into his shoving or shaking her violently until she stopped pressing him.

Whether his wife was really as unsympathetic to Bob's being tired as he portrayed her or not is beside the point here. What is important is that Bob's way of handling a fairly common domestic situation was to choose a blunt "go to hell" response to his wife and follow it with physical violence if she did not retreat immediately. It achieved his immediate goal of getting her to leave him alone but was becoming more and more destructive to their marriage. In the therapy sessions Bob appeared intelligent and willing to learn new strategies for handling his own anger as well as his wife's evident frustrations. Both Bob and his counselor did not take the naive view that tensions and anger-provoking situations would never arise again. Rather, Bob had to learn new techniques for dealing with them. He also had to learn a new set of values that would make violence against his wife unacceptable *to him* as a solution to their disagreements.

Another important set of characteristics of these batterers included their occupations and income. Most men in our study were blue-collar workers, working in factories as machinists, driving trucks and buses, working on construction crews, doing carpentry or brick-laying, and so forth, or they held low-paying white-collar jobs such as public school teaching or clerking. Their average (median) income was $15,000 or less. (Again, doctors and lawyers batter women as well as men working on assembly lines, but their wives tend not to choose the shelter option to deal with the problem, as we will show in Chapter six.)

These two factors, poor education and low income, have enormous impact on the violence that occurs in the homes of women who turn to a shelter for help. As we saw in Chapter two, about half the wives of these men were full-time homemakers, often having modest formal education themselves and part-time jobs requiring few skills if they did work. Thus the incomes of these families did not give them much of a buffer against economic pressures. Most of these young men were in occupations where job availability can fluctuate widely. The precarious economy of the early 1980s and the fact that so many of these men were in precisely the types of jobs hardest hit by the recession suggests that we are looking at a part of the male population most susceptible to outside strains and pressures. At the same time they were men least able to find alternative, nonviolent ways to cope with these problems.

The role of economic strain in aggravating family violence, making it either more severe or more frequent or both, particularly in young families where the man is struggling to establish a comfortable home for himself and his family, is undeniable. Unemployment among these batterers was about 15 percent, more than double the highest unemployment rate in the Dallas–Fort Worth area during the two-year period of our study. Moreover, unemployed batterers scored higher, on the average, on our Severity Index than did abusing men who were employed. A story appearing in a local newspaper around the time we were finishing this analysis examined the connection between the declining state of the economy and family violence. It told the case of one woman whose common-law husband had been unemployed for eight months. The woman told the reporter:

> I was still working, but just part-time. So we were both always at home. He'd be real mad, usually it would be on payday after I'd bring my check home. He'd be real mad, and say, "Just because you're working..." Then it would start. He'd hit me with his fist, he hit me on my stomach. I was pregnant, and he wanted me to have an abortion, but I didn't want to. He threw me against the wall, pushed me down the stairs. Things like that.

The man's frustration and even embarrassment that she worked while he didn't is obvious. The woman eventually had a miscarriage caused by his abuse.[2]

Note, however, that we have been careful to use words like "aggravate" when talking about economic pressures and violence. The consensus of virtually all family violence experts on the role of economic pressure is the same as on the role of alcohol and drugs: such factors do not cause the violence, but they make it easier for it to happen. This is why so many battering instances started over surprisingly trivial matters, such as the woman's habit of biting her nails, her particular choice of lipstick, or what happened to be served one night for dinner. These were not the real causes, but they could serve as the sparks to ignite an already angry man. Similarly, economic pressures can give the man an excuse to batter, or they can make a bad situation worse by increasing his frustration. Thus Mary Morrison, executive director of the National Coalition Against Domestic Violence, in speaking of how the worsening U.S. economy was making domestic violence a more severe problem nationwide, warned:

> We see some relationship between an increased number of calls and increased unemployment. But our analysis of those situations say they were instances waiting to happen . . . It's a mistake to say, "Oh well, he lost his job, that's why he's beating her." The kind of man who is going to beat her will sooner or later anyway.[3]

The ethnic backgrounds of the batterers reveal an interesting pattern. It is a cliché in the field of family violence that such violence cuts across all class and racial or ethnic boundaries in American society, that it is the preserve of no one group or type of person. True enough, but does it occur across these boundaries equally? In Chapter two we showed that Caucasians, blacks, and Hispanics were found among shelter women in about the same proportions as in the larger population. This was also true of the batterers. Moreover, they tended to marry racially and ethnically similar partners. We wondered, however, if the severity of the batterers' violence was the same for the different ethnic groups. In other words, was the violence committed by batterers in one ethnic or racial group likely to be as severe as in another?

Reviewing past studies, we found that virtually nothing was known of racial or ethnic differences in family violence. Research on family violence is simply too new to have delved into such questions yet. We decided to compare four racial/ethnic groups of batterers to see if there were differences in the severity of their violence as measured by our Severity Index. We discovered that the groups were not the same. Black batterers were more likely to have used very severe violence on women than were Hispanic batterers. The latter in turn were more likely to have been seriously violent batterers than either white-Anglos or the groups we called "others" (native Americans and Orientals).

This is a potentially important finding, but one that many people might misinterpret. After all, race and ethnicity are sensitive topics, and enough stereotypes of battered women already exist without our creating more. For example, racial/ethnic differences in the severity of violence do *not* mean that black men in general make more violent husbands or lovers, or that white husbands in general treat their mates better. But in practical terms these differences show that black women were more likely to have been severely beaten when they arrived at shelters than either Hispanic or white-Anglo women. One reason is that black and Hispanic women were more likely to be in lower income families than white-Anglo women, and therefore more often lacked the resources to escape violence that white women possessed. As a result, these minority women found it more difficult to leave the home until the abuse became extreme, even life-threatening. At the same time, men in the minority families in our sample were the most likely to be exposed to economic strains outside the home, which often caused heightened abuse. In the case of black Americans, sociologists have long observed that black women are frequently employed while their husbands or boyfriends are not. This type of situation adds an element of friction to a relationship already strained by poor economic conditions. Particularly in the cases of dependent, possessive men, which many batterers unquestionably are (as we saw from the women's testimonies in Chapter two), the fact that the woman earns regular wages while the man does not, regardless of who spends them, would be an aggravation.

A final but important characteristic to be considered about the batterers is how general were their violent tendencies. Did they confine their violence to their homes, to their wives and children, or did it spill out and affect others? Was the man beating his family members exclusively, using them as an outlet for his antisocial frustration, while in other respects a decent, respectable citizen?

It appears otherwise. Almost nine out of ten men were violent toward children, animals, and physical objects, and not just to their mates. (See Table 4-2.) They destroyed property, not just in emotional rages but also with a cold disregard for the rights and feelings of others. Sometimes they used this kind of violence to create emotional havoc that merely hitting another person could not achieve. Some men directed their anger at valued possessions of women as a way of hurting them. One husband deliberately bought his wife paintings and art objects, then during quarrels would methodically smash and ruin them in front of her as "punishment." A few men we learned of smashed only things they knew the women had bought, for the same reasons. Another husband let his wife decorate the Christmas tree with meticulous care, then deliberately turned it upside down and shook all the trimmings off later when his wife became angry at his coming home drunk late on Christmas Eve.

Cruelty to the family dog seemed to be common in many homes. Household animals frequently became targets for men's rage. Battered women witnessed a sad succession of family pets eventually taken to veterinarians' offices to be treated for broken bones and cracked teeth or cuts. Ironically, dogs would sometimes have to be destroyed for the inevitable "meanness" that they developed after long periods of such mistreatment.

Nor were these batterers model citizens outside their homes. *Over 80 percent had arrest records.* (See Table 4-3.) This is obviously an unusually high proportion of men who have been in trouble with the law, and it shows the unsavory character of men who force women to seek safety in Texas shelters. The

limited amount of research done by others on seriously battering men shows a similar pattern of criminality.[4] Not counting
the assaults on the women in the shelters, committing violence against other people had led to arrest of one out of four
of the batterers.

In summary, our emerging portrait of battering men is not
flattering. We readily admit that it is not representative of all
violent men. We find few bank executives, surgeons, or successful politicians in their ranks, although we know through other
sources of prominent Texans in those categories who batter
their wives. In much of our study, the violence seems to have
been affected by the economic vulnerability of the families:
their relatively low levels of education, their modest (even mar-
ginal) incomes during an inflationary recession, and the fact
that they are generally one-income families with a number of
young children.

It is a grim fact that by this point we are no longer talking
about violence limited to adult women. Findings from Chapter
three on the problem of child abuse and the additional evidence
discussed here show that these men are violent individuals inside as well as outside their homes: they attack wives, children,
pets, household objects, even strangers. Even if these men are
not typical of all batterers in society, they still have to be taken
into account, for we know that they have driven women and
children into shelters. And there is no reason to believe that
men like these will go away or their numbers will shrink in the
foreseeable future.

WAS THE BATTERER HIMSELF A VICTIM
OF CHILDHOOD FAMILY VIOLENCE?

Though batterers are only now beginning to be systematically
studied, there has been a fair amount of speculation as to what
makes them so violent. Predictably, such speculation has followed the theoretical biases of the observers. Psychiatrists, for

example, see violence toward family members as an expression of insecurities and neuroses caused during early life. By beating a woman, a man is actually rechannelling some early infantile hostility or fear of a parent toward her. Psychiatrist Leroy Schultz maintained that his research on men who tried to kill their wives showed that such men transfer their dependency needs from their mothers to their wives but then lash out when the wives cannot and will not meet these needs.[5] Another author reasoned that boys need to overcome their unconscious fear of being feminine and go overboard in the opposite direction by acting out the role of "super male." [6]

Social psychologists do not usually accept the sexual assumptions of psychiatry, but they also emphasize that early life experiences are important in shaping adult behavior. Currently the most fashionable social psychological explanation of battering is the generational transfer hypothesis, which we conclude is not very successful for explaining women's victimization (see Chapter two.) English women's advocate Erin Pizzey has stated this view succinctly:

The man who is violent comes from a home where there was violence and dreadful unhappiness. He tries to compensate by creating a home of his own as soon as possible... Usually the first beating occurs on the honeymoon because the man is still a damaged child who reacts to any stress with total explosion, and what was a temper tantrum at five is a lethal act of aggression at twenty-one.[7]

Sociologists Straus, Gelles, and Steinmetz similarly concluded:

Each generation learns to be violent by being a participant in a violent family. We traced this learning process through three generations. The more violent the grandparents, the more violent the couples in our study are as husbands and wives, and the more abusive they are to their children. The children of these couples, in turn, tend to follow the pattern of their parents.[8]

In fact, these authors write of a double effect for some children: they witness violence between their parents and are physically abused as well, giving them the greatest probability of becoming a violent husband, wife, or parent.

Sociologists at times agree with both psychiatric and social psychological explanations, but their emphasis is more on social factors outside the family that impinge on its members. One of the most obvious sources promoting violence is the cultural tradition and attitude condoning or even glorifying it. A number of authors have made the often repeated observation that our entire western sexist tradition, from our laws to our romantic literature and media images, has made, in sociologist Murray Straus's words, the marriage license unfortunately also a hitting license for men.

Much of the feminist writing on family violence argues the same point. While many authors see a lessening of wife-battering as a hoped-for long-term effect of sexual equality, the short-term effect may be the opposite. Pressures for this equality, particularly in the working world, may increase family violence, not decrease it. This is because male superiority is still the dominant ideology in our society. As a result, social changes such as gains for women in legal rights and employment opportunities, which are bringing about greater equality between the sexes, cause strain and frustration for males expecting to retain their traditional authority. The logical outcome is increased violence by men against women.

Undoubtedly the most important concept underlying most of the sociological research on family violence is stress. Some research deals with how factors such as income and education enable the different socioeconomic classes in American society to cope with stress that originates not among family members but in the economy. Straus, Gelles, and Steinmetz examined the relationship between stress and family violence by presenting husbands in their national study with a list of eighteen potentially stress-producing problems, such as "laid off or fired from work," "arrested or convicted of something serious," "spouse became pregnant," "sexual difficulties," "big increase in housework or responsibility on the job," "child caught doing something illegal," and so forth, asking respondents to indicate which of these misfortunes they had personally experienced in the past year. They found economic and employment stress to be major contributors to family violence.

One reason for the current popularity of explanations involving stress is the lack of mind-reading needed. Objective measures of income and formal education are relatively easy to obtain, compared to more subjective information on how a man was raised or what his unconscious needs really are. Obviously so far we have drawn heavily on the objective approach, explaining characteristics about men and women that contributed to their violent relationships.

But so-called "stress" factors, whether economic or some other kind, only point to influences that might make family violence worse, that is, more severe or more frequent. They do not really deal with its causes. The generational transfer hypothesis, on the other hand, does attempt to get to the roots of such violence. Since it is so often referred to, but rarely backed up by facts, we want to give it particular attention. We looked at what was known of violence in the childhood homes of the men in our study. The results tell us some important things about the origins of male battering. (See Table 4-4.)

- Six out of ten batterers witnessed physical violence between their parents.
- Four out of ten batterers had been neglected by their parents as children. Four out of ten batterers had been physically abused by their parents.
- One out of every three of the batterers' brothers and sisters had been abused by their parents. Moreover, in two thirds of the childhood homes where the batterers had been abused, their brothers and sisters were as well.
- Gauged by our Severity Index, batterers who were abused during childhood were the men most likely to abuse their own children.

These patterns show substantial (though not complete) support for the generational transfer hypothesis *among men*. It is obvious that a considerable number of these men grew up in violent homes where they were not the only victims of violence. We do not suggest that they learned to enjoy it, or that they learned to enjoy inflicting it on others. We do think that as they grew up these men came to accept violence as normal and (at least as far as beating women was concerned) proper for males.

If the women's retrospective descriptions alone confirmed the generational transfer hypothesis, we might not have much confidence in this explanation. Yet the high rates of abuse of the current generation of children, which we reported in Chapter three, strengthens the argument that a noticeable core of batterers are reliving their childhood tragedies by beating and frightening their own children. If anything, it is likely that the shelter's resident women, when interviewed, underestimated the amount of childhood abuse which the men in their lives had endured.

The same can be said regarding the alcohol-related problems of the batterers' parents. In over one out of five cases the batterer's mother was believed by her daughter-in-law to have a drinking problem. Almost half the fathers had drinking problems. It is possible, of course, that the women reporting these patterns may have only recalled (or heard of) instances when one or both parents-in-law were violent and drunk, and we have no independent knowledge of whether or not either of the parents was indeed a problem drinker. Nevertheless, alcohol and violence appear to have been linked. The fact that the shelter residents also reported 60 percent of the current batterers as having alcohol or drug-related problems, plus the fact that these substances were frequently involved in beatings, plus the unlikelihood that any of the shelter residents had ever heard of the generational transfer hypothesis, point strongly to an intergenerational connection.

WHAT IS THE BATTERER'S REACTION
AFTER A VIOLENT EPISODE?

The shelter residents were presented with a list of possible reactions that their husbands or boyfriends might have had immediately after beating them. (See Table 4-5.) Since most women were beaten repeatedly over a period of months and years, we would expect one of two reactions. One would be psychologist Lenore Walker's three-stage cycle of violence: a build-up of tension, the beating, and then a "honeymoon" phase when the man goes to the opposite extreme of acting very affectionate and caring. This is obviously a way of keeping the woman from leaving the relationship and restoring the appearance of a happy home. A second reaction might be the opposite: the batterer feels that beating his mate is his God-given right as a male and sees no need to apologize for his violence. He is, in short, unrepentant.

Almost half the batterers acted affectionately, following the Walker model, and sometimes did favors for their wives after violent episodes. Two thirds of the men apologized to the women when it was over. Such an about-face had a tremendous effect on women torn between staying and leaving, raising hopes yet again about the possibility that the violence might finally end. "Honeymoon" was the most frequent term used when we asked women how far the men went to make amends to them. "It was like we first got married again," one woman remembered. "He gave me gifts, was nice to our daughter, we went on trips, and the sex was great." At the very least this behavior caused the women great ambivalence. Psychologists Karen Coleman and Paula Howard of the Texas Research Institute of Mental Sciences interviewed dozens of women who had been in violent homes and concluded that many women use this "honeymoon" behavior to help keep an optimistic image of their marriage and a sympathetic picture of their mates alive. Such statements as, "He would never hit me if he didn't drink" . . . "He is so affectionate after the fights" . . . "I feel sorry for him because he has so many problems," reflect this attitude.[9]

This honeymoon behavior by men also caused some women to become protective of the batterers. As Coleman and Howard noted:

> Many of the women in our study said they had felt "crazy" for staying in the relationship but were reluctant to talk about violence with anyone other than a close friend or family member. Others were protective of their spouses. As one woman said, "I love my husband more than I can tell and it really hurts me and makes me feel terribly guilty to talk about him to a complete stranger." She had attempted to solve the problem by physically separating from her husband for short periods. She estimated that she had left him 26 times in seven years, once had attempted suicide, and was currently taking a tranquilizer.[10]

Thus there is some reason for the man to show this behavior. But a more ominous statistic was the other response. Half the men felt the battering was justified (even if they apologized), an obvious indication that the violence would very likely occur again. *It was also in those families where the men felt the beatings were justified that the violence was most severe.* Men who believed they had good reasons to beat women scored higher on our Severity Index than men who reacted differently after violence. Thus not only does the frequency and duration of violence increase along with the husband's or boyfriend's feeling that it is his right to "discipline" the woman, but the severity of the beatings also increases.

How do battering men justify their violence against physically weaker women? Often the answer seems to be the same reason stronger, larger parents give to explain why they discipline children: because they need it to behave correctly. Many women were apparently told what one woman, the bruises from her husband's fists still visible on her arms as we interviewed her, related: "He said a household has to have a head, and he was the one. He was the man, so it was natural. If I didn't like it, I could find another home."

A separate, in-depth study of marital violence among seventeen couples conducted at Houston's Marriage and Family Clinic of the Texas Research Institute of Mental Sciences helps provide a further glimpse of batterers' essentially sexist justifications. Below are several brief excerpts of discussions among batterers, their wives, and therapists on the topic of how striking the women supposedly would make them into better family members:

MR. R.: I just don't like to have to go through that, you know, but I have to bring out my points or try to bring out to her the things that could be better or beneficial to the whole family if she would just change her ways.

Mr. R. went on to explain that he viewed physical force as a justifiable way to handle family arguments.

MR. R.: I'm never worried about the after-effects because I'm never ashamed of anything I do or say. I never have been.

THERAPIST: You mean when she had the black eye, you didn't mind?

MR. R.: That's right. Because I would not have given her that black eye unless something would have made me give it to her.

MRS. R.: But I have seen the times when I have been bruised and he told me it made him feel bad.

MR. R.: I will feel bad about it, but I won't regret it and there are two different things to that part of it. Feeling bad about it, but I would never ever done it if I didn't have a reason, so therefore I'm not ashamed of anything I did.

Another man in the Houston sample talked of hitting his wife in order to keep his three-year-old son from getting upset:

MR. P.: She is likely to start an argument when we go to bed. She would start out whispering and get louder and I'd tell her to shut up and that would make her mad and she would get louder. I don't want her to wake the boy up because when he sees us arguing or fighting, well, he, the kid, starts crying and jerking and I don't want him to get woke up like that so I usually hit her or something, you know, just to tell her to shut up, before she, you know, wakes him up.[11]

We also must recognize that some men combined reactions; that is, they played out "Jekyll-and-Hyde" performances after abusing women. One ex-shelter resident visiting a shelter (she said it was "the only place I feel completely safe anymore" even though she had moved out of town) while we were interviewing women recounted her former husband's regular postbattering routine:

He became very emotional when it was all over. I mean he came unglued. He sobbed and cried and begged me to forgive him, to take him back. It was pathetic, it was so heartrending. At times like that he actually made me feel guilty and I felt better after I forgave him. Then the same day, maybe only hours later, he'd stop being grateful or apologetic. His other routine would start. He'd get cool about it all. He'd tell me that women's place was to get beat up in fights. He'd say he knew it was wrong, but the world had a double standard. The world was unfair. If we wanted to live in it we had to accept sexism, inequality, and all that. He'd start thinking up things I had done to anger him. We were back to square one.

Men would sometimes exhibit these turnarounds in incredibly brief periods of time. One resident felt it was still the "weirdest" aspect of her abusive husband:

He called just yesterday afternoon. He knows I'm still in the city, but he doesn't know where. It's bugging him to no end . . . he's been out in his pick-up looking. He wanted me to give him the shelter's address so he could come and talk to me. I said I wouldn't so he called me some names and said he would kill me. Then he asked about the kids. Finally he asked if we could still be friends and go out dancing this weekend. He's horny. God! I couldn't believe it!

Psychologists and battered women themselves have repeatedly noticed the abusive man's dependency on the woman. She is the target of his rage, but as the above example illustrates, he also needs her. Ironically, need and anger become so thoroughly intertwined that the man himself often becomes blind to how he switches from one emotion to the other. Eventually this erratic pattern produces a tragic attitude in some battered women. Often during their stays in shelters they become distrustful, not just of the abuser but of all men. It is not a feminist attitude but rather a bitter, cynical approach to the entire opposite sex. "All men are potential batterers," a woman told us matter-of-factly. "And under the right conditions most men will be abusive." She no longer felt she could take a chance believing otherwise.

These men may not have transformed the women to whom we talked as are traumatized, shock-numbed dogs of psychological experiments, but they have stolen a precious thing from many women, perhaps permanently. It is the conviction that men and women can live together and produce something better than what either one of them alone can have: a growing, loving relationship.

THE BATTERER AND FAMILY VIOLENCE

The batterers round out our picture of what occurs in family violence. In a sense they are the center of the problem, not just in woman-battering but also in child abuse. True, we know that women commit child abuse as well as men, but it is the men who most often decide that violence is to be a way of life in the home. They do this through sheer brute strength. If we had studied a group of batterers truly representative of all levels of society, the family violence picture would be more complete and undoubtedly also more complex. Still, the fact that the research available on middle- and upper-class family violence shows so many similarities with our findings suggests that we can generalize from this study.

Violence is a family affair in more ways than one. It is a problem that affects each member differently. Women find their roles as homemakers, workers, and lovers completely overshadowed by their role as victims. They cannot be effective mothers when they must add self-defense and even self-preservation to their daily activities. Impressionable, vulnerable children cannot develop their own potential when what should be a nurturing, supportive environment turns into one of tension and terror. The reactions of men after the beatings, and particularly after the women leave the homes, reveal that their lives too are distorted by the effects of violence.

No family is capable of handling continuous serious violence, least of all the lower-middle-class family we have analyzed. The precarious incomes, educations, and occupational skills of the men and women; the presence of vulnerable young children; the men's reliance on force and their frequent acceptance of it: these factors often need only a catalyst such as a poor economy to raise the level of violence to a point where the women feel they must run for their lives. More important, no society can survive in any meaningful way if its most fundamental institution is torn apart by internal violence. In an impersonal, highly technological society the family is supposed to be a haven, a place where violence is locked out. Instead, we see that, ironically, more and more homes are becoming places where violence is locked in, and people are literally breaking out to search for havens.

Violence is also a family affair in another way. We have seen that it is an inheritance bequeathed from one generation to another, both directly and indirectly. Others have made the same claim, but we now have a clearer idea of how it happens. Serious batterers are very likely to have been abused and neglected children themselves, growing up in homes where the father and mother quarrelled violently. A sexist culture, which glorifies this violence in its entertainment, its humor, and its literature, reinforces the lessons learned at home. In turn, these men are likely to abuse their own children either deliberately or because they lack knowledge of any other style of parenting; some know better, some do not. Most carry their violent upbringing into other areas of their lives as well, running afoul of the law and hurting people outside the home. We have reason, based on what we know of three generations' experience with violence, to expect that a high percentage of the boys in our study will be abusive men by the end of the century. Also, based on what we have seen of their fathers, many will become criminals or earn police records as well. But their violent behavior will be only the most visible, tangible effect of the abuse and neglect they've experienced. We cannot even begin to estimate the serious emotional side effects that will stay with many of them the rest of their lives.

5

AFTER THE BATTERING: A WOMAN'S OPTIONS

Battered women feel a range of emotions after experiencing violence in their homes. Some cling to the hope that their men will change, particularly if there is an affectionate honeymoon phase that follows. Some women simply accept abuse as part of their marriages. Some flee in panic or after careful deliberation.

But it is not simply a question of staying or leaving. Either option carries with it several alternative courses of action that a woman might choose. In this chapter we want to discuss frankly, and what at times may seem cold-bloodedly, just what these alternatives are. They range from the woman deciding to make the best of her relationship with the violent man to ending the abusive relationship altogether. Not every alternative will be equally acceptable to every woman. Some we would not advocate under any circumstances, though women do take them. Yet a woman in a violent home has to make a decision about what she is going to do, not only for her own best interests but sometimes also for the interests of her children. They cannot take the initiative to leave or seek help unless they are teenagers, so it is up to her. We believe a discussion of all the courses of action open to a battered woman may help her, or someone who cares for her, find the best way to improve her situation.

THE OPTION TO STAY

Most people create homes with at least some sense of commitment. Even nonviolent homes have their stormy periods. Women who discover they have married or are living with an abusive man have many reasons to want to stay. As we have seen, some men give conflicting performances that confuse women, making them unsure what to believe about their relationships. Or a woman may interpret the man's domination of her as a sign of his affection. Some women may have religious beliefs that tell them it is shameful to divorce, or believe that escape from a violent home is desertion. Many women feel they are not able to leave because of financial hardship. They have no jobs, little money, and small children for whom they are responsible. At one conference on woman-battering a speaker summed up the issue of staying in abusive relationships as she asked the women in the audience:

> Have you ever stayed in a relationship longer than you should have? Was it because of a sense of failure on your part? Or a feeling of responsibility for the other person? Did you stay because of the children? Were you afraid of loneliness? Were you fearful of your ability to make it in the big, bad world?[1]

Whatever her reason for staying, however, a battered woman should know the realities of various ways of coping with violence if she decides to stay.

Passively Enduring the Violence

No one knows how many women in violent homes decide simply "to stick it out" indefinitely, but it is probably a large number. These are the invisible majority of battered women.

True, we are seeing more women coming into shelters and divorce courts who once might have taken abuse passively but who now no longer feel it is part of a woman's natural lot. However, there are indications that many women are still willing to live in an abusive home. For many it is a cultural problem. For example, a recent survey of teenagers funded by the National Center for Prevention and Control of Rape and conducted at the University of Southern California found that over half the young men felt they were justified in forcing a young woman to have sex if, in their opinion, she had flirted with them or "led them on" but then refused to go further. Just as important, almost half the young women expressed the same opinion.[2] The feminist movement may have received a lot of attention in the media and may have affected college-educated women, but apparently its overall impact on many young persons is limited.

After a talk on family violence one of us gave to a community group, a woman came up to the speaker's rostrum to defend woman-battering "within limits." Since our research has generally brought us into contact with the opponents, not the champions, of family violence, it is worth briefly noting her reasoning. Her name was Joan, and she had been married to a batterer for 15 years. She was a 36-year-old housewife and the mother of three children. She had never had a job other than homemaker, having married after attending a Texas "bible" college for two years. Joan was a deeply religious woman. Her husband's violence had been more sporadic and more severe when they were younger, but as the children grew older and she learned ways to "steer clear of his bad moods" the violence leveled off to relatively mild forms, mainly slaps and shoving. She told us:

> Now the only time he gets a little rough is when I do something wrong. Like the other day when I went by to visit with my mother across town and didn't tell him about it first. My mother has been sick for a long time now and I

was the only one around to look in on her... I learned a long time ago the things that make him mad. [Such as not telling him that she went out to visit her mother.] So he gets a little rough. But I forgive him. I really do believe that the man should be the head of the family, though. That's what it says in the Bible, and I believe in the Bible.

In many cases, though, the violence does not level off. It grows progressively more severe. In fact, of the women in our sample the most severely abused women were also the ones who had been beaten the longest and most frequently. Thus, any woman who has been hit or shoved or hurt physically in any way faces a strong likelihood that in the future such violence will happen more often and may become more serious. Passively enduring is sheer martyrdom, but the reward will have to be claimed in heaven. Things will not automatically "take care of themselves" or clear up down here.

Contacting a Clergyman

The sad fact is that ministers and priests are currently much better at marrying men and women than they are at dealing with spouse abuse and domestic conflict. While we know (based on our study of several thousand Hotline telephone calls to the Family Place) that some ministers did refer battered women in their churches to the Dallas shelter, we have yet to talk to a woman who felt she received much aid from a clergyman. A number of women were quite bitter about their futile attempts to get clergy to help. This is not surprising. Recognition that family violence is serious and wide-spread, not a freak problem, has been slow in coming in all sections of American society; the clergy are no exception. Learning to counsel families with this problem is not a regular part of seminary training; courses in pastoral counseling do not normally deal with assault, incest, and rape.

Just as important, the clergy have traditionally had powerful reasons to minimize family violence as a problem in their congregations. The family is, after all, the bedrock underlying most churches; families, not individuals, are their typical membership units. To confront violence in an otherwise respectable family reflects poorly on the mission and ideals of a church. It also reflects indirectly on the effectiveness of the minister as the shepherd of his flock. Family violence also seems scandalous, something that is too lower-class and disturbing to be dealt with comfortably in many middle- and upper-class churches.

The situation can be better or worse, depending on the denomination or church to which the woman belongs. Based on our conversations with family violence victims, women in Roman Catholic, Greek Orthodox, and conservative Protestant churches (such as the Church of Christ, the Southern Baptist Church, and various fundamentalist denominations) are most likely to find their priests and ministers of little help. The kinds of family conflict that might lead to divorce or separation threaten these groups. Their clergy are likely to recall the admonitions of Saint Paul on controlling women and use them to justify telling the woman she must stay in the abusive home. Here women will probably be counseled by a minister to "try to be a better wife" or to "be more considerate of him" and "obey him." Leaving the abusive man, or divorcing him, will be branded desertion or a sin, shifting the blame to her.

In short, if she is a church-going battered woman her chances of getting meaningful ministerial help are better in churches of a more moderate-to-liberal persuasion such as Methodist, Presbyterian, Episcopalian, or Unitarian. The lack of help from clergy is regrettable but true. Clergy offer one of the largest groups of professionals who can potentially deal directly with domestic violence, but a clergyman's willingness or ability to help an abused woman is still more dependent on his personal knowledge and opinions than on training in the problem. But clergy can learn to recognize the signs that violence is a problem in the homes of some parishioners. They can become aware of the pressures on both men and women that cause it. And they can recognize the dangers it poses to all members of the family as well as to the family institution. But until such time as re-education takes place, abused women can expect little real help when they turn to the clergy for advice if they wish to stay in a violent relationship.

Calling the Police

Often, after hearing a story of domestic violence, people will respond, "But why didn't she call the police?" This seems like an obvious course of action. After all, the law enforcement profession exists to contain and prevent the sorts of serious violence we have been describing. But the blunt truth is that the police usually do little more than stop an actual fight in progress. They may offer to escort a battered woman safely out of the house and drop her off somewhere else, but they cannot make peace in the home or solve the problems between spouses. Most of the time they will not arrest a violent man, *and in a surprisingly large number of cases they may not even show up after the woman has called for help.*

In our research we analyzed the cases of 2,096 women who had called Dallas's Family Place shelter for help within a two-year period and found that only 45 percent had ever called the police because of domestic violence. This figure is significant, since one of the police's foremost complaints about domestic violence is that answering such calls accounts for so much of their time (time, they imply, that could be better spent on more "serious" crimes). It further suggests that the police would be virtually swamped with domestic disturbance calls if all or most women being beaten telephoned them for assistance. As it is, less than half the women who finally flee their homes have called the police. (See Table 5-1.)

Even more revealing figures emerged from our study of the telephone calls. According to these women, the police responded to their calls only 69 percent of the time. (See Table 5-2.) That means that in one out of three cases the police did not even show up! In examining the 380 of the 2,096 cases where we had more detailed information, the pattern was the same. One in three calls by the women went unanswered. Only

20 arrests of the men were made. These arrests occurred only when the woman was visibly, seriously hurt (cut and bleeding, for example) or when the man threatened the police and/or became violent to the woman in front of them. Police officers told 39 women "they could do nothing" and referred only 14 to the Dallas shelter. In 50 percent of the cases the police gave advice to the women that was essentially useless. Women were frequently told such things as:

- Why don't you file a report?
- Why don't you just leave for a while?
- Have a cup of coffee and cool down.
- We can't get involved in family business.
- Why don't you two try to talk things out?
- Why don't you go back to your family?
- You don't seem hurt now.
- He says he's sorry.
- Lady, we aren't marriage counselors.

The lack of police effectiveness in treating woman-battering as assault is a sore point among both abused women and shelter workers, for responses such as these are common. However, we do not mean to portray the police as villains. (In Chapter seven we will deal specifically with their viewpoint on this problem.) They find it frustrating to answer domestic disturbance calls and encounter women who expect them to sweep the men away to jail with no due process, or women who have had second thoughts after calling the police station and decide not to press charges. They resent sometimes risking their lives to break up violent quarrels and then seeing the wife suddenly become protective of the abuser when she goes to court. They grow tired of having to return repeatedly to the same home, like referees in a boxing match, while the man and woman are doing nothing to get at the source of the problem. Domestic disturbance calls are time-consuming and nerve-straining, and even handling them successfully or effectively brings little of the professional prestige to police that apprehending more traditional criminals does.

For the abused woman wondering if the police can help her, past experience points to some practical limits to what they can do. She should remember that the police don't want to get involved in domestic violence, they won't always get involved even if called, and they probably can't resolve it when they do arrive at a home. In short, they are no solution to the problem. If a woman feels her life is in danger, then by all means she should call them. They *can* provide temporary protection. The odds that they will respond to her call are better if she is threatened with a weapon and if she lives in a middle- or upper-class neighborhood. On the other hand, if she has called the police before because a man is beating her and did not press charges against him, the odds that they will respond are worse. (One shelter director told the Texas Senate Subcommittee on Human Resources at a public hearing, "If a woman has locked her violent husband out of the house and he is trying to break in, we tell her not to tell the police on the phone that it's her husband. She should say it's a burglar.") But unless the woman is willing to press assault charges against the man, there is little the police will do in most cases. They will not make the man leave because it is his home too. He will have to be violent in front of them or to them or have a previous outstanding warrant for there to be an arrest. If they do arrest him, he will often be out of jail within a few hours, probably angrier than he was before.

There is a better chance that the police will respond or arrest a violent man if a woman has obtained a peace bond or a temporary restraining order (TRO), but these have mixed effectiveness. A peace bond requires the man to put up a certain amount of money, which he forfeits if he breaks his peace with a woman. A TRO is good for ten days and, by the time court costs are added up (even without a lawyer), is also expensive to the woman who must pay to obtain it. A TRO is an *ex parte* legal document issued by a judge, meaning that a man does not have to be present when a woman files for it (though he is notified of it later by the court). If he violates a TRO's instruction to stay away from a woman, she can take him back to court for having violated the order. Of course, the available legal remedies vary from state to state, with some states having no provisions for such aid.

Some women reported that TRO's did intimidate violent men, or that police would arrest men if a TRO was produced while the man was still in the home. However, many men slip away before the police arrive. Other women said the TRO made no difference; that the police saw no evidence of any harm and refused to make an arrest. Still others said their furious husbands simply tore up the TRO's, and when the police arrived there was no proof of their existence. Some legal experts have lobbied to have a record of TRO's and peace bonds in police computers so that the police would not simply have to take a woman's word that the man was acting illegally by being back in his own home. But such computerization is still relatively rare. Even Austin, the capital of Texas, does not yet have such a program.

TRO's have other limitations. They generally are not available between 5 P.M. Fridays and 8 A.M. Mondays, the period when much domestic violence occurs. In addition, in Texas as well in several other states a woman has to file for divorce to obtain a TRO; if she has decided to stay in the relationship she might not even consider this action. If she does file, even through the state-supported Texas Legal Services, the cost starts at $104, and there is a week's lag between initial interview with a lawyer and serving the papers. Also, a TRO must be continually renewed to be effective.

We know of one case of a woman (through her attorney) who did use the courts creatively to get police response and reform her abusive husband by filing for divorce, although she had no immediate plans to leave him. Unfortunately the story had a tragic twist. Mrs. B.'s husband (a construction worker), whom she loved, was a violent man as well as an alcoholic. As time went on his drinking became worse and he began creating extra problems for the family by writing bad checks and damaging its credit. In a desperate attempt to impress on him his need for treatment and her unwillingness to put up with more violence, she filed for divorce, convincing him to waive his rights to attend any hearings. He did respect the TRO and ceased being violent toward her. Using the legal document as her shield, she convinced him to seek treatment for his drinking problem, which he also did. Afraid that he might backslide, and as a reminder to him that resuming his former habits would be enough to make her leave, she went ahead and divorced him. All this time they had never stopped living together. Their relationship improved as Mr. B. straightened out his problems and stopped drinking. And neither the neighbors nor the three children had any idea that Mrs. B. had filed for, and won, divorce from Mr. B. She had used the courts to end the man's violence and preserve the relationship. Unfortunately, *one week* after the divorce had been finalized Mr. B. was killed on the job largely owing to his company's negligence in following safety precautions. Mrs. B. filed for Mr. B.'s insurance, but the insurance company refused to pay her, claiming she was no longer his wife.

Mrs. B.'s plan backfired, but it illustrates two things. First, it shows the lengths some women are willing to go to stay in abusive relationships and work to improve them. Second, it shows the limitations of the legal system for helping battered women.

Choosing a Violent Resolution

In several shelters we asked women directly, "Did you ever consider killing your husband?" Surprisingly, many replied that they had considered such an act. One south Texas respondent recalled, "I remember staring at him passed out on the sofa, snoring. I thought of going into the kitchen and getting a big knife and sticking it in his throat." Why didn't she? "Then I thought, where would I go, with two little kids? If I went to jail for murder, what would happen to them?"

In one of our discussions with a group of women in a shelter, every one admitted to at least having let the thought of homicide enter her mind. A few had let it go beyond that when they were being abused, but had not found a lethal weapon handy. Most had rejected the idea as a serious alternative when they realized the consequences for their children. None seemed to feel the long process of standing trial or the possibility of prison was the main deterrent. One woman remembered:

> He was over 200 pounds, twice as big as I am. I would beat back at him with my fists, which only made him hit me back harder. If I had had the strength, or a gun, I would have killed him.

A large-boned, six-foot-tall former schoolteacher told us:

> He was a big man, six foot four and way over 200 pounds. But I always felt if someone hit me I should hit him back twice as hard ... One night when I wouldn't take drugs with him he pushed me down onto the floor. That infuriated me. I pulled the phone out of the wall with a tremendous effort and smashed it into the side of his head. It tore open a gash along his jaw. He was stunned but more shaken by it than I was. It occurred to me later that I could do that to him when he wasn't looking.

Like the first woman we quoted, some women realized the abuser's helplessness when he slept, particularly when the man was in an alcoholic stupor after a violent episode. One woman considered taking a pillow and smothering her husband but was afraid he would wake up. Several considered stabbing the men.

However, none of the shelter residents had ended their abuse by disposing of their mates. While many had fantasized about it at some point, some more seriously than others, they did not act out such violent daydreams. They chose to leave rather than meet violence with violence.

Yet some women do stop the cycle of violence with the supremely violent act of killing the abusing man. We certainly do not advocate this solution to the problem of woman-battering, but it is nevertheless an alternative that women have used, and one that is gaining legal credibility.

We began Chapter one by summarizing the case of Francine Hughes, a battered woman who set her home ablaze while her husband slept and who was later acquitted of his murder by reason of temporary insanity. Hers was an exceptional case. But it had much in common with other murder trials involving domestic violence. Judges and juries are typically ignorant of the extent of the domestic violence problem in this country and cannot understand why any sane woman would voluntarily remain in a violent relationship if she is not literally imprisoned. They have little comprehension of, or empathy for, the condition of a woman trapped in a violent home. As Delores Jiminez, a clinical psychologist, has stated, most people are insensitive to the emotional trauma the woman is going through, and underestimate the amount of fear involved. Fear immobilizes and often restricts the woman from reaching out for help.[3]

While writing this book we served as consultants and expert witnesses in the legal defense of two Dallas–Fort Worth area women who shot and killed their husbands. Both had been physically and sexually abused for several years, both were married, and both stood trial for murder in the fall of 1982. Since the following details are matters of public record, we have used the actual names involved.

In April 1982, 24-year-old Tammy Byrd shot her husband, Dwight, with a shotgun at close range in their Dallas apartment. He had been mildly abusive before their marriage, splitting her lip or bruising her cheeks in arguments, but afterward he became increasingly more violent. His slaps turned to punches, and he began sexually abusing his wife by tying her up and forcing her to "experiment" (in particular, forcing oral and anal sex upon her). When she resisted he would beat her and threaten her with knives, bayonets, and loaded guns, which he kept under and around the bed. It was not unusual for Tammy's twin sister to visit and find her sleeping on the floor of the bedroom closet or in the bathroom, having locked herself in for the night. One Christmas Eve Dwight confessed to a longtime friend that he knew he had a problem, for he had earlier threatened Tammy by pointing a loaded gun at her. He said he was worried that he might "lose control" and kill her.

In late April 1982 Dwight beat Tammy especially severely with a belt when she refused to have her wrists tied. Then he tied her up as usual and brutally raped her. After that incident she vowed he would not mistreat her again. One night not long after this, when he did in fact try to repeat his coercive routine, she refused. Dwight had been lying naked on the bed. As he rose Tammy pulled one of Dwight's many weapons, a loaded shotgun, from underneath the bed and warned him not to hurt her. Dwight replied that if she did not use the gun on him he would use it on her. Then he lunged at her. Tammy thrust the barrel forward, turned her face away, and fired point-blank into his body. He died almost immediately.

The defense attorney, Michael Gibson, enlisted us to explain to the jury how a woman could be trapped in a violent relationship and feel that she could not leave despite seemingly having many opportunities to do so. He wanted us to put this incident into perspective by educating the judge and jury about the pervasive problem of wife abuse in the Dallas–Fort Worth region.

After various witnesses, including law officials, had testified to Dwight Byrd's history of violent encounters with the police and drug dealing, and after Tammy's emotional recounting of how her marriage had degenerated into a sadistic nightmare, Stacey took the witness stand. However, not far into his testimony the prosecuting attorney objected that the facts Stacey cited were irrelevant to the Byrd case. Without personal knowledge of the defendant, he maintained, Stacey could only speak directly about 542 other women, who were not involved in this case. His objection was immediately sustained by the judge. Stacey was permitted to finish his testimony, but with the jury removed from the courtroom. (Defense attorney Gibson wanted a comparison of the Byrd case with the data from our study put into the court record in the event that he had to appeal a guilty verdict. At the appellate court level he knew this information would be considered.)

Ironically, though the jury never heard Stacey's testimony, there is good reason to think it had a positive effect. The jury members knew that expert testimony pertinent to domestic violence had been denied them because it would have put the defense's case in a more favorable light. Since none of them presumably knew much about the extent of the problem of family violence, they undoubtedly realized that what Stacey had to say might have weighed toward acquittal. The vehement objections of the prosecution only reinforced this realization. Moreover, the defense attorney, who knew virtually nothing about domestic violence before the trial, had been coached by us on what arguments to use in explaining the climate of fear in Tammy Byrd's life shortly before she killed her husband.

The jury took less than an hour to acquit Tammy Byrd of the murder charge and declared she had acted in self-defense.

Not long after the Byrd trial we were asked to serve as expert witnesses for the defense in a similar case. This was a much more sensational trial, involving prominent local figures, heavy publicity, courtroom theatrics, and scandal. Richard "Racehorse" Haynes, a well-known, flamboyant Houston trial lawyer, was the defense attorney. This case also revealed much about the criminal justice system's current inability to understand or deal with the domestic violence problem.

On July 23, 1982, Pamela Ruth Fielder shot her husband seven times with a .45-caliber automatic pistol in their Fort Worth home. He was a prominent local gynecologist; she managed her own real estate company. It was the second marriage for both of them. Pamela was tried for murder twice, the first ending in a mistrial when it was learned that the prosecution had not provided the defense with all the information concerning the shooting. What emerged from testimony during the two trials was a sensational story of sadomasochistic abuse and violence. From courtroom testimony and our own conversations with Pamela Fielder, leaving out all but the most basic elements, we can give the following account of the case:

Pamela Fielder and her first husband, a career military officer, divorced over the fact that he desired natural children and she, for medical reasons, was unable to have any. Her second husband, Dr. Darwin Fielder, was a Fort Worth gynecologist who (by her account and from evidence presented in the trials) became increasingly fascinated with sadomasochistic sex. Since this involved a good deal of pain for both of them, he used his physician's knowledge of drugs either to prolong stimulation or to deaden the pain for both of them. When Pamela refused to go along with his demands, he would beat her with his fists and feet. His sexual interests included bondage (she claimed he would achieve an erection simply by snapping a handcuff on her wrist), sadism (court photographs showed he had pierced her nipples and labia with metal rings), masochism (he had once nailed his scrotum to a board; she also claimed that when he tried to do the same to his foreskin the first hammer blow caused him to ejaculate), and eventually scatology (a preoccupation with human excrement). It was this last perversion, according to her, that led Pamela Fielder to decide to seek a divorce.

The prosecution claimed that Pamela shot Darwin out of jealousy when she learned that he was having an affair with another woman, which he was. The defense claimed that though she had learned of the infidelity shortly before the shooting she had nevertheless already intended to divorce her husband. After she told her divorce attorney about Darwin's perversions, he advised her to collect what became referred to during the trial as Darwin's "sex toys" (two leather whips, metal manacles, a black lace-up hood) from the "cave" (a special locked closet where they were kept and where Pamela said she had been hung for hours in handcuffs when she resisted his sexual demands). Before she could gather these articles and take them to her lawyer, she was confronted by her husband. She then told him she wanted a divorce and also that she would reveal his bizarre sexual tastes. According to her he became enraged, and she had to kill him in self-defense.

There were no witnesses, so no one except Pamela Fielder knew for sure what had happened in the Fielder home on July 23. The prosecutor was forced to base his case on circumstantial evidence, such as Pamela's hysterical ramblings immediately after the shooting and the presence of more than one ammunition clip near the gun (implying that she had emptied one clip, already partially empty, and taken the time to reload and shoot Darwin more times, hence murdering him in cold blood). At the conclusion of the second trial, the jurors (the majority of whom were men) found her guilty, not of murder but of voluntary manslaughter, a less serious crime in Texas carrying a punishment of 2 to 20 years in prison and a $10,000 fine. The fact that she had used a weapon made it likely that she would be denied early parole. As we were finishing writing this book Pamela Fielder's attorney was appealing the verdict and she was free on $5,000 bond.

We had Pamela Fielder fill out a Texas Department of Human Resources shelter intake form identical to the ones we obtained for the 542 women in our study, and from it we calculated a Severity Index score for her that we could compare with those of the shelter women. Her score ranked in the 98th percentile, or, as Shupe later explained to the judge in her trial, only 2 percent of the men in our study were more violent than the late Darwin Fielder.

Shupe testified first, and things proceeded very much as they did in the Byrd trial. Not far into his testimony the prosecuting attorney objected, on the grounds that the material from the larger study was irrelevant to this particular case. Defense attorney Haynes countered by pointing out that Shupe had met with Mrs. Fielder prior to his testimony and could put her particular claim of self-defense into better perspective using sociological research. The judge delayed ruling on the objection, had the jury leave the room, and allowed Shupe to reply to

Haynes's questions about the findings before deciding if the jury should hear the material. Uninterested and clearly impatient to eliminate this (from his viewpoint) purely academic jibberish, the judge ruled that the testimony could only appear in the court record (where an appeals court might see it) but could not be presented to the jury. Shupe was dismissed as an irrelevant witness. In an attempt to at least impress upon the jury the fact that expert opinion was being deliberately disregarded, Haynes then called Stacey to testify and history repeated itself. Stacey too became irrelevant.

Lawyers deal in specifics, while sociologists deal in trends, so the fact that our testimonies in both trials were ruled irrelevant for technical reasons is understandable. What would seem to the average person important in making sense of human motivations in a violent situation (the Fielder trial, like the Byrd trial, was really over the question of motive; neither woman denied killing her husband) did not fit the legal rules of what is admissible evidence. It is tempting to decide cynically that many of those rules were set up to create more orderly trials and for lawyers' convenience rather than to bring about justice or help reveal truth. It is also difficult for us as nonlawyers to know if the legal status quo will change. But combine the present legal view of the relevance of outside evidence with the overall lack of awareness of the scope of domestic violence (even in professionals) and you have the following scenario: Unless a jury is convinced the murdered man was totally reprehensible (as in both these cases) and the woman had no other possible motive than self-defense (as in the Byrd case), *conviction of murder or voluntary manslaughter is likely.*

In the current legal system, unless jurors are individually aware of the domestic violence problem before they enter a courtroom, they may determine guilt or innocence in these cases on the basis of personal prejudice and stereotypes about why women remain in violent homes. The realities of the woman's dilemma in particular can remain something mysterious and inexplicable to them. This was never more clear than when the jurors in the Fielder trial were interviewed the morning after it was over by a reporter from the *Dallas Morning News*. They reported that all the sexual aberrations of the dead man, the beatings, his threats, and the humiliation which prevented Pamela Fielder from leaving her husband and eventually caused her to shoot him made absolutely no difference to them. By their own admission, the abuse was the least important factor in their decision. For example, referring to the overwhelming evidence of Darwin Fielder's violent personality, juror Dani Livingston, an actress and director, said, "That was seen through readily. We decided that it didn't matter." [4]

Thus, unless new ways to introduce social science research into courts are found, jurors will have no answer to the obvious question they naturally want to ask: "But why didn't she just leave?" Meanwhile, killing the abuser, however necessary in self-defense, is a dangerous alternative for a battered woman. The criminal justice system is too unenlightened about domestic violence to recognize the self-defense motive on a consistent basis.

Contacting an Outreach Program for Women

A relatively new type of service for women that Dallas's Family Place now offers and that other shelters are considering is a counseling program aimed at women experiencing physical abuse but who nevertheless feel they can salvage their marriages. It is an option midway between simply enduring violence and jettisoning the relationship. It operates more as an "outpatient" service than as a residential facility. In Dallas this agency is in a different location from the shelter but is run by the same nonprofit corporation that runs Family Place. This center offers us a glimpse of battered women who are from different backgrounds than the typical shelter resident.

In Dallas this program is referred to as the Help Center. By March 1982, 67 women had used its services. Most were middle class or above and around 30 years old, therefore better off financially and slightly older than the average shelter woman.

The typical Help Center woman earned a personal income of slightly over $15,000 a year (most were employed outside the home rather than as homemakers), while their husbands' average salary was over $20,000 a year. In short, these were middle- and upper-class women with substantial investment in their homes and who, aside from the violence, had considerable inducements to stay.

But this also means their reluctance to leave their homes was not (as it so often was among shelter residents) because of limited resources. Nor were they reluctant to leave because their beatings were less severe than those of lower-class shelter residents. In fact, the abuse they suffered was often more severe than that of the shelter residents (although not quite as frequent). What is more, sex abuse was more often reported by Help Center clients, though it is of course possible they were simply able to recognize it. (See Tables 5-3 and 5-4.)

Then why did these women choose to become involved with a counseling center rather than leave their abusive relationships? As we have seen, many came from affluent homes that they were reluctant to leave. Two-thirds said that one reason for coming to the Help Center was simply for moral support. Over half claimed to need counseling to help cope with violence. One in three said she needed information about the kind of violent situation she was in and what could be done about it. (See Tables 5-5 and 5-6.)

In other words, what these women said they needed, and what the Help Center provides, is a source to which they can turn when trying to handle the implications of violence in their families. The Help Center gives them encouragement, practical survival skills to handle everyday strains that can trigger violent situations, and the chance to meet other women in families that they want to maintain if violence can be stopped.

Such specialized services for women are not yet as common as resident women's shelters. This reflects the newness of the concept of shelters and the priorities that we mentioned in Chapter one. Life-threatening situations for women with fewer resources must be dealt with before the predicaments of women with more options. But as awareness of the different needs of different women in various situations mounts, and as agencies specialize to meet these particular needs, we can expect many such help centers to be established across the country. These are not welfare projects for the rich. Nor are they cheap substitutes for divorce lawyers. In fact, if the television evangelists, right-wing politicians, and other self-appointed advocates of the American family really want to keep families together in the face of contemporary pressures, they will think seriously of encouraging women to seek out such places and find ways to see that these centers are financially supported.

THE OPTION TO LEAVE

The battered woman's decision to leave her own home shows desperation. It means things are so unpleasant, even dangerous, that any safe place is preferable to home, despite the loss of possessions and perhaps even luxuries. But if a woman does make up her mind that it is time to get out, she still faces decisions. There are the questions of where the best place is to go, whether she is leaving the man permanently, and how she will survive financially and emotionally. Of course, what is best for any individual woman is ultimately her decision to make. There are several possibilities that need to be considered by a woman thinking about leaving. First, however, we will discuss a way to help a woman decide whether she will leave at all. Then we will list some options if she does decide to leave.

Deciding When to Leave

Whether to leave her home or stay is certainly no easy choice for any woman to make. Most women want their marriages to work, and most batterers probably do too. The ambivalence that results can often cause a woman in a violent home to lose perspective and underestimate just how serious things can eventually become. The severity of the violence she experiences is an important factor in her decision. For this reason we developed a special questionnaire with a very practical purpose in mind.

We call it the CSR (Center for Social Research) Abuse Index. We designed it to help a woman or anyone else gauge just how violent (and dangerous) a domestic relationship is. The questions are all based on the patterns of violence that have emerged from this study and other family violence research. It is short and can be filled out quickly. It is easy to compute a score. Moreover, the final score can be compared to a chart displaying four possible levels of abuse. Thus, the Abuse Index allows a woman (or a friend) to estimate the level of danger she may be in. It can be a constructive aid in helping sort through her options.

CSR ABUSE INDEX
ARE YOU IN AN ABUSIVE SITUATION?

This questionnaire is designed to help you decide if you are living in an abusive situation. There are different forms of abuse, and not every woman experiences all of them. Below are various questions about your relationship with a man. As you can see, each possible answer has points assigned to it. By answering each question and then totaling these points as directed, you can compare your score with our Abuse Index. You will know if you are living in a potentially violent situation, and if you are abused, you will have some estimate of how really dangerous that abuse is.

DIRECTIONS: Circle the response to each question that best describes your relationship.

1. Does he continually monitor your time and make you account for every minute (when you run errands, visit friends, commute to work, etc.)?

Frequently	Sometimes	Rarely	Never
3	2	1	0

2. Does he ever accuse you of having affairs with other men or act suspicious that you are?

Frequently	Sometimes	Rarely	Never
3	2	1	0

3. Is he ever rude to your friends?

Frequently	Sometimes	Rarely	Never
3	2	1	0

4. Does he ever discourage you from starting friendships with other women?

Frequently	Sometimes	Rarely	Never
3	2	1	0

5. Do you ever feel isolated and alone, as if there was nobody close to you to confide in?

Frequently	Sometimes	Rarely	Never
3	2	1	0

6. Is he overly critical of daily things, such as your cooking, your clothes, or your appearance?

Frequently	Sometimes	Rarely	Never
3	2	1	0

7. Does he demand a strict account of how you spend money?

Frequently	Sometimes	Rarely	Never
3	2	1	0

8. Do his moods change radically, from very calm to very angry, or vice versa?

Frequently	Sometimes	Rarely	Never
3	2	1	0

9. Is he disturbed by you working or by the thought of you working?

Frequently	Sometimes	Rarely	Never
3	2	1	0

10. Does he become angry more easily if he drinks?

Frequently	Sometimes	Rarely	Never
3	2	1	0

11. Does he pressure you for sex much more often than you'd like?

Frequently	Sometimes	Rarely	Never
3	2	1	0

12. Does he become angry if you don't want to go along with his requests for sex?

Frequently	Sometimes	Rarely	Never
3	2	1	0

13. Do you quarrel much over financial matters?

Frequently	Sometimes	Rarely	Never
3	2	1	0

14. Do you quarrel much about having children or raising them?

Frequently	Sometimes	Rarely	Never
3	2	1	0

15. Does he ever strike you with his hands or feet (slap, punch, kick, etc.)?

Frequently	Sometimes	Rarely	Never
6	5	4	0

16. Does he ever strike you with an object?

Frequently	Sometimes	Rarely	Never
6	5	4	0

17. Does he ever threaten you with an object or weapon?

Frequently	Sometimes	Rarely	Never
6	5	4	0

18. Has he ever threatened to kill either himself or you?

Frequently	Sometimes	Rarely	Never
6	5	4	0

19. Does he ever give you visible injuries (such as welts, bruises, cuts, lumps on head)?

Frequently	Sometimes	Rarely	Never
6	5	4	0

20. Have you ever had to treat any injuries from his violence with first aid?

Frequently	Sometimes	Rarely	Never
6	5	4	0

21. Have you ever had to seek professional aid for any injury at a medical clinic, doctor's office, or hospital emergency room?

Frequently	Sometimes	Rarely	Never
6	5	4	0

22. Does he ever hurt you sexually or make you have intercourse against your will?

Frequently	Sometimes	Rarely	Never
6	5	4	0

23. Is he ever violent toward children?

Frequently	Sometimes	Rarely	Never
6	5	4	0

24. Is he ever violent toward other people outside your home and family?

Frequently	Sometimes	Rarely	Never
6	5	4	0

25. Does he ever throw objects or break things when he is angry?

Frequently	Sometimes	Rarely	Never
6	5	4	0

26. Has he ever been in trouble with the police?

Frequently	Sometimes	Rarely	Never
6	5	4	0

27. Have you ever called the police or tried to call them because you felt you or other members of your family were in danger?

Frequently	Sometimes	Rarely	Never
6	5	4	0

To score your responses simply add up the points directly below each question's circled answer. This sum is your Abuse Index Score. To get some idea of how abusive your relationship is, compare your Index Score with the following chart:

120–94	Dangerously abusive
93–37	Seriously abusive
36–15	Moderately abusive
14–0	Nonabusive

A woman with a score of 0–14 lives in a nonabusive relationship. The sorts of strains she experiences are not unusual in modern homes, and she and the man deal with them nonviolently. A woman with a score in the 15–36 range, however, definitely does live in a home where she has experienced some violence at least once in a while. It may be that this is a relationship where the violence is just beginning, or perhaps for whatever reason it has stopped at this level of severity. But in a new relationship there is good reason to expect it will eventually escalate into more serious forms and may occur more frequently.

Women with scores in the 37–93 range are in a seriously abusive situation that can, under outside pressures, or with the sudden strain of a family emergency, move into the dangerously severe range. In a seriously abusive situation serious injury is quite probable if it has not already occurred. Much of this abuse is assault, pure and simple, by a violent man. A woman here needs to consider finding counseling, talking the man into counseling if he will accept the idea, or sorting things out after going to a shelter. She should seriously consider getting help, even leaving.

Women with scores in the top range of 94–120 need to consider even more seriously the option of leaving the relationship at least temporarily (and possibly soon). The violence will not "take care of itself" or miraculously disappear. Over time the chances are very good that the woman's life will literally be in jeopardy more than once.

Going to a Hostel

Youth hostels in various countries are safe, clean, and relatively inexpensive places for young travelers to stay overnight. The concept of a hostel is that it is a place offering temporary shelter for people passing on after resting there. We can think of a battered woman leaving home and finding a room in a motel or the YWCA or a cot at the Salvation Army as staying in a sort of hostel. In the short run it puts a roof over her head and she is safe from abuse, but it is not a real solution. It can also be expensive. More important, hostels are never equipped to help an abused woman decide what options are best for her. They are in the business of providing temporary shelter, not attending to the many emotional, physical, and economic needs of women who leave abusive homes. A woman should by all means choose this option if things become so bad in her home that she feels her life or the lives of her children are in imminent, serious danger. But she then should be prepared to face the harder decision of where to go next.

Going to Friends and Relatives

The problem with leaving an abusive man and going to friends' homes is twofold. First, her friends are often his friends. Married people tend to socialize and build relationships with other married people as couples. If the abuser is domineering and possessive of a woman, as many are, then she may not have any immediate close friends who would not be torn between their friendships for her and him.

Even if she does have a friend she can rely on, the battered woman runs up against a second problem. In the blunt words of a famous piece of folk wisdom: "Fish and guests smell after three days." In many cases, then, going to friends' homes can present the same obstacles as going to a hostel. And this can be just as true of relatives as friends. There should be a strong enough bond among family members for them to help a battered woman in an emergency, but she may feel embarrassed or ashamed or be afraid they will blame her or tell her "I told you so."

But are the fears that a woman conjures up in her mind really justified, or can she rely on friends and relatives for help? Our research indicated that they *are* positive resources, that people the woman knows outside the home, whom she may never have thought of turning to, do care about her personal welfare. In analyzing 2,096 Hotline calls made to Dallas's Family Place we found that one out of every three calls was not from a woman seeking help, but rather from her friends and relatives. In addition, one out of every ten calls came from employers, co-workers, apartment managers, or neighbors, who had seen the shelter's telephone number in the newspaper or the phone book or on television.

All of these individuals were concerned about the safety and welfare of women who they knew were in violent domestic relationships. They made the effort to find out what could be done to help her in her situation and to extend her options. While the woman, not her friends or family, must make the decision to come to a shelter, the fact that they are supportive enough to help her explore ways to deal with her problems should give her encouragement.

An abusive man will often denigrate a woman. He may tell her she is ugly, incompetent, or worthless. Often he will tell her she has no choice but to remain with him, that no other man would want her and no one else will help her. Many women have told us they had begun to believe the man, and did not leave because they believed they could not. Brenda, now a university undergraduate in her mid-twenties with a preschool-age child, never entered a shelter. We met her in one of our classes. Her case conformed to much of the published literature on wife abuse. Her husband was violent when drunk and exhibited the classic honeymoon behavior after an episode. He was possessive of her and deliberately kept her isolated from anyone he did not trust. With no employment outside the home, she had no access to her own money. She felt she could not turn to her parents because they had disapproved of the marriage in the first place. Her mother-in-law told Brenda to accept his behavior, that his father was the same way. Brenda finally decided that she had to leave. She began removing small amounts of money from her husband's billfold after he had fallen into a drunken sleep and (in her words) "squirreling it away in a jar back in the closet." But after nine months she still had no idea of where to go or what to do. Finally Brenda received a letter from an aunt who had never occurred to Brenda as a person to call. She telephoned the aunt. The aunt had no idea that Brenda had been living in a violent situation and immediately volunteered her spare bedroom for an indefinite period. That offer gave Brenda the resolve to do what she had been planning for months. The next Saturday, when her husband went out early in the morning for his usual golf game, Brenda rented a trailer, had it hitched to her car, loaded it herself, and was gone.

Unless a woman and man have managed to conceal violence totally, the chances are very good that someone, or even a number of persons, close to a battered woman may suspect her problem and will be willing to help. For her sake they should tell her this.

Getting a Divorce

Getting a divorce is more than just a legal procedure for a battered woman. It can be an ordeal during which she must hide or stay on the move to evade an angry, violent man. Ordinarily a divorce entails living at least six months (at least in Texas) formally separated from the man. But if the divorce is her idea, he may not make this easy. During this period many batterers come after the woman, for despite their mistreatment of her they need her desperately. To many of these men temporary restraining orders mean nothing. They can become so emotional over the idea of her leaving that their mood when they do find her is foul and murderous. One jealous, angry husband broke into a south Texas shelter the weekend before we visited it, looking for his wife (who was not a resident there). He ran through the halls terrifying the women and children, smashing out windows and kicking in doors. Another Texas shelter has a thick steel front door scarred and pock-marked from hammer blows. This kind of reaction to a divorce is not unusual among violent men.

Therefore, a battered woman who considers a divorce may need to be prepared to sit out the waiting period in living arrangements unknown to the batterer. If he is truly a jealous, possessive person, there is also a good possibility that he will not consider the relationship over when the divorce is finalized.

A divorce is simply a legal recognition that two people's marital relationship and obligations are severed. It says nothing about the emotions that may still exist. Regardless of the law, the batterer may not regard the woman as free. He may even want revenge. More than one woman divorced from an abusive man has told us of receiving threatening telephone calls months after they were legally no longer man and wife.

From the standpoint of the health and safety of both women and children, a divorce is unquestionably the best course of action for the more serious cases we have seen. Whether it would be the best for less violent families has to be decided by the woman, depending on her belief in the man's capacity to change.

ANOTHER COURSE OF ACTION

Just because a woman leaves her home to escape violence does not mean that she will not return or that her marriage will automatically end in divorce or that the man will not become less violent. Frequently she needs time to assess her life and situation somewhere where anger and hostility do not constantly impinge on her thoughts. If she has no money or immediate family nearby she needs a place to go, where she can live and perhaps keep her children with her. She needs a place to gain the necessary perspective to guide her in what she does next about her relationship with a man. It must be a place more permanent than a hostel but less permanent than a home. It should be a place sympathetic to her need to leave an abusive relationship but not committed to encouraging her to end it.

Such a place is a shelter, another course of action possible once the option to leave is chosen. We will consider shelters, their realities and potentials, in more detail in the next chapter.

6

ANOTHER ALTERNATIVE: SHELTERS FOR BATTERED FAMILIES

Shelters in which women and their children can find safety, away from the menace of a violent male, are extremely recent developments. There were fewer than 10 shelters in the United States at the end of 1974, but 79 shelters by 1979. In many states they are barely two or three years old, yet they continue to expand and multiply in the face of a seemingly inexhaustible public demand. In 1982 Texas had 36 operating shelters, 29 of them supported in part by state funds, with over two dozen more starting up.

In light of both the "venerable" history of domestic violence in this country and twentieth century America's overall commitment to human and civil rights, it may strike some persons as surprising that the shelter movement took so long to arrive. Nevertheless, it was not until the late 1970s, when rape crisis centers, Salvation Army havens, and other social service agencies began to be inundated with battered women desperate for temporary physical sanctuary, that local communities as well as state bureaucracies began to explore ways to cope with this newly recognized problem. The movement started slightly earlier in England, where Erin Pizzey, a woman with no formal background in social work or counseling, took it upon herself in the early 1970s to establish "safe houses" for battered women and children. These shelters were and are completely run in democratic fashion by the women who live there communally.

The lack of professional staffing distinguishes the English shelters from their American counterparts. In the United States social workers and other members of helping occupations have been quick to add the problems of family violence victims to their professional mandates. Thus there is a marked distinction in most of the hundreds of American shelters between staff and residents.

Few persons have a clear picture of what a women's shelter is like, what a woman experiences when she goes there, and how she is treated. Many women fear that they will encounter "blaming the victim" treatment from callous bureaucrats, or, if their children have also been mistreated, that they will be blamed and the children taken away. They fear that the shelter will automatically pressure them to seek a divorce from the batterer, or that they will simply be processed by an unfeeling, inhuman state agency. Many who have seen the overcrowded, spartan conditions of a Salvation Army mission understandably want no part of any similar environment. Some women are afraid they will be considered welfare recipients, their dignity further degraded. Few women, it is safe to say, fully understand the larger purposes and the many services that shelters nationwide are now being staffed and funded to provide.

At the same time there is an incredible amount of ignorance among our highest public officials regarding shelters. Many politicians have a totally incorrect view of such places, believing them to be hotbeds of anti-male, anti-marriage, and anti-family attitudes. Shelters have been accused of breaking up families and causing divorce. Perhaps the most sexist charge is that they exist only to provide lazy, pampered housewives with a place to go when they want to run away from their family responsibilities.

Nothing could be further from the truth. Leaving an abusive family situation and choosing temporary residence in a shelter is one option open to a woman confronting violence, and as an option it deserves to be considered realistically in view of the costs and benefits entailed. We will begin with a description of the founding of shelters, using the example of Texas.

THE ORIGINS OF TEXAS SHELTERS

The first shelter in Texas opened its doors in June 1977 in Austin, the capital. It received an immediate response from women in that community. By August 1981 the Austin Center for Battered Women was not only regularly filled to capacity but was having to deny shelter and protection to many people. In that month alone, over *600* women and children had to be turned away.[1]

History repeated itself across the state during the next few years. The momentum was accelerated by House Bill 1075, which the sixty-sixth session of the Texas legislature passed in 1979. This bill allocated $200,000 to be divided among six new shelters, one of which was Family Place in Dallas (its share amounted to $50,000). The funding was to last only ten months. This proved to be an important piece of legislation, because it indicated the first official recognition that family violence was a growing problem. The law mandated the Texas Department of Human Resources to contract with family violence shelters to:

1. Provide protection and temporary shelter in a family oriented environment for victims of family violence and members of their families until the victims may be properly assisted through counseling, medical care, legal assistance, and other forms of aid.
2. Reduce the high incidence of deaths and injuries sustained by law enforcement officers in handling family dis-

turbances and to aid law enforcement officers in protecting victims of family violence from serious or fatal injuries.[2]

As the second half of this mandate shows, much of the official recognition of the problem came from police concern that growing family violence increasingly put *them* in dangerous situations. The victims of such violence were only part of the motivation behind the legislation. However, in the fall of 1980 Representative Mary Polk introduced Texas House Bill 1334, which would provide more permanent shelter funding. The following January the legislature passed it, giving family shelters the expectation of more stable support, although the state was limited to funding 75 percent of each shelter's operating costs and actually funded only an average of 23 percent. This legislation allocated $900,000 for 1982, $1,050,000 for 1983, $3,839,495 for 1984, and $4,393,900 for 1985. The number of shelters correspondingly grew from 6 in 1979 to 36 in 1982; plans call for 40 shelters by 1984 and 45 by 1985.[3]

The previous few paragraphs, however, don't tell the more human side of how the shelter movement spread (and continues to spread) in Texas. It is largely a story of gutsy female social workers and counselors, aided by some male allies, struggling to convince the people who control public and private purse strings that victims of family violence could no longer be ignored. It involved thousands of hours of effort (and just as many miles of footwork) by women such as Debby Tucker and Eve McArthur, former directors of the original Austin shelter, in lobbying senators and representatives, contacting state bureaucracies, and raising public awareness through the media. Though a few sympathetic, far-sighted officials such as Representative Polk and Chet Brooks, chairman of the Texas Senate Subcommittee on Human Resources, were indispensable in obtaining the necessary legislative commitment to funding family shelters, setting up such shelters was largely a grass-roots achievement. Every shelter has its own unique history, with separate individuals who made creating a viable, permanent shelter their personal crusade. A brief look at how Family Place took shape out of the original concern and perseverance of determined citizens will give a better sense of how the shelter movement has grown during the last half-decade.

THE FAMILY PLACE STORY

In many communities one person or a small group of persons becomes alarmed and disturbed enough to mobilize resources to help meet the needs of victims of domestic violence. In Dallas, Texas, the single person probably most responsible for community awareness of domestic violence and for leading the creation of Family Place was a woman named Gerry Beer. Vivian Castleberry, a Dallas journalist who followed the local shelter movement during its early struggles, wrote of her:

> She has become one of the most effective volunteers in the city of Dallas. At a time when volunteerism is unpopular in some circles with women feeling pressured into a paying career, Gerry has already been full circle. She has worked, quit to rear a family, returned to work successfully for more than three years and has now returned as a full time volunteer.

Gerry Beer described the sort of philanthropic spirit that motivated her to become a shelter advocate during an interview with Castleberry:

> My training tells me that I shouldn't work for nothing, but the ultimate goal is worth it. People are suffering and when people hurt, they are in no position to fight their own battles. Somebody who has the time must be willing to take the criticism that goes with doing what has to be done. I have the time and the means and I must! [4]

This was not the first time Gerry Beer had worked as a volunteer. She had learned and practiced many of her organizing skills working to get parents more involved with their children's schools and the community. Her involvement with domestic violence began after meeting an attractive, intelligent young professional woman who had been its victim. Gerry Beer was shocked to hear a story not unlike many we've related throughout this book and then to realize that countless other women were experiencing the same thing, with nowhere to turn for help. Her commitment grew when she saw other women in Dallas about that same time petitioning the city council for a shelter but bungling the effort because of inexperience in community action programs. She realized that the first step was to obtain the support of the right individuals and groups in Dallas and to obtain private monies, with few strings attached.

Using her previous experience, her contacts with city officials, and the advice of her husband (a well-known Dallas realtor), she began amassing broad support. Her coalition included wealthy philanthropists from prominent families, such as Anne-Marie Cadwallader, Betty Graham, and Helen Hunt; a local judge, clergy, and people in the medical community; and organizations such as the Dallas branch of the National Conference of Jewish Women, a local Methodist church, the city's Junior League, and the Organization of Business and Professional Women. Other existing social service agencies lent their support and cooperation. Grants from private sources, in particular the Dallas-based Hoblitgelle Foundation and the McMurray Foundation, were eventually secured.

Out of these efforts came the nonprofit Domestic Violence Intervention Alliance, Inc. (DVIA). On February 28, 1979, the DVIA opened the doors of Dallas's first shelter for battered women. Even at that time there was a realization that women would not be the only clients. This is one reason that DVIA chose to be a sponsoring organization, separate from the shelter. Family violence in general, not just spouse-battering, was to be the wider focus of its concern. Likewise, Gerry Beer had seen the suspicion of conservative officials that such shelters might be subversive to the family, encouraging spouses to divorce. She therefore pushed for the shelter to be called The Family Place, avoiding any implication even in the name that the shelter served only women or did not deal with the larger family problem.

The original Family Place was a dilapidated two-story house, which was immediately filled to capacity and which stayed that way. Only days after its opening women who called for help could not be housed because of lack of space. Family Place staff were forced to adopt a policy that only those women in serious life-threatening situations would be accepted as residents. Other women had to be referred to other agencies, which in most cases could not meet their needs adequately. According to Gail McIntosh, DVIA executive director since the original shelter opened, during that first year 200 women and 400 children found refuge in Family Place where, in her words, they were "given time and space to consider alternatives in a safe place." Many more had to be turned away.

In November 1980 Family Place was able to move to a new location (a former medical clinic), thanks primarily to the generosity of Anne-Marie Cadwallader. Journalist Castleberry described it at the time:

> The new house is on a tree-shaded block in a residential area of Oak Cliff. It has 12 bedrooms, several with lavatories in the rooms and some sufficiently large that movable partitions have been added so that women can have privacy while sharing a room. There is a foyer at the front. On the left is the hotline lounge where all incoming calls are processed. To the right are three supervisory offices. A conference room provides space for group meetings and counseling. A play room for the children, a large laundry room, a kitchen with all appliances and a miniature cafeteria complete with the house which is more than double the size of the old one. The house accommodates 16 women and remains full all the time. At present the residents are mothers of 24 children.[5]

The new shelter is more than twice the size (and twice the capacity) of the first residence, yet Family Place has been full virtually since the day it opened. Only women whose lives are in immediate danger can enter, sometimes escorted by the police, without being placed on the waiting list. By the spring of 1982 this list averaged 80 new women a month. It is easy to understand the constant need to reshuffle names on the long list and the pressures for services put on the shelter staff. In one year's time almost 1,000 women will have to be put on waiting lists, and most of these will never be admitted. To put it bluntly, they were not being beaten badly enough. With the average two children per woman, in a year approximately 2,000 children are involved. *Three thousand women and children seeking help from a single shelter during a single year, and most were denied it.* Extrapolating to the entire state of Texas offers us a grim picture. The national implications are mind-boggling.

THE SHELTER'S SERVICES

The Domestic Violence Intervention Alliance, Inc., which is chartered to oversee Family Place's operation as well as that of the Help Center, has a board of directors made up of 30 people. Their professional backgrounds vary, but all share a common concern with the problem of family violence. The board is divided into eight committees that supervise such things as fundraising, long-range planning, educating other professionals in the community about family violence, recruiting and maintaining shelter staff, maintaining the shelter physically, and working with Dallas churches. For the most part, however, the board of directors leaves the day-to-day running of Family Place and the Help Center to DVIA's executive director and the shelter's associate director.

Family Place offers a number of services to families. There are, of course, the most obvious needs: housing, food, and safety from the abusive man. In addition, a number of services are provided to women once they have entered the shelter. Some need legal advice, whether it concerns criminal prosecution of the batterer or starting divorce proceedings. Some women require medical treatment. Many need jobs, which also involves the problem of finding some regular means of transportation. If women want to establish living arrangements apart from the batterer they usually require deposit money to rent an apartment and help in apartment hunting. When women have suddenly left their homes in the middle of the night, without time to prepare for a stay at the shelter, they may have left children's schoolbooks, medication, or other things with the violent man. The shelter can arrange for a woman to return home with a police escort to get them. The shelter tries to meet these needs and a host of others, such as providing toys and extra clothes for children. Therapy and workshops for groups and individuals, women and children, are held regularly. If child abuse has occurred, Child Protective Services will be contacted.

Family Place also operates the 24-hour-a-day crisis Hotline where trained counselors talk with women or their friends by telephone. If a case is urgent in terms of saving the woman's life, the counselor may arrange immediate admittance to the shelter. If not, the counselor can put a woman on the waiting list. Counselors screen a large number of miscellaneous calls that are made by women looking for divorce lawyers, child support payments, alcohol rehabilitation, food stamps, and cheap overnight lodging. Referrals are made for these women to other agencies in the city. Occasionally a man claiming to be the victim of his wife's battering will call, and these men too are referred to appropriate counselors.

One reason the Hotline counselors field calls from women with so many different problems is that people who refer women to Family Place have various ideas of just what a shelter's purpose is. Particularly on weekends or at night, after most nine-to-five social service agencies have closed, the Hotline is one of the few places women in trouble can call. Thus, it is not unusual that hospitals, medical clinics, police, and the Salvation Army (to name just a few) refer battered and nonbattered women alike to Family Place.

The shelter staff splits its responsibilities for providing these services into six programs, each with a separate coordinator who reports directly to the associate director. There is a coordinator of women's services, of children's services, of ex-residents' services, and of volunteer staff members. There is also a coordinator of shelter management (or house manager) and a separate coordinator of the Help Center.

Volunteers make up the largest proportion of the staff. In the fall of 1982 there were 56 volunteers in all, assigned to work under one of the five shelter program coordinators or under the Help Center's coordinator. These volunteers come from all walks of life. Some are former shelter residents now committed to curbing family violence through the shelter movement. Some are businessmen, housewives, or students. They come from civic organizations such as the Junior League and church groups. The Dallas Volunteer Center, which acts as a clearinghouse for volunteers, provides many. So do Family Place's media advertisements. Word of mouth is also an effective recruiting device.

Gail McIntosh summed up what the shelter aims to do for battered women in a newspaper interview:

> Our goal is to save lives and to provide women the safety and resources they need to determine their future plans . . . Residents are encouraged to work toward creating a healthier climate with their husbands whenever possible . . . Our program works. We give women a safe place. We provide a climate where they can work at raising their self-esteem. They learn that they are valuable, and that they have the right not to be hurt and that they have the power to make choices. Then we show them the available community resources for taking charge of their lives and teach them how to get the services. There could be almost perfect options for them but if our residents do not know about them, the services would be worthless.[6]

LIFE IN THE SHELTER

We asked various women in several shelters to go back in time, asking them to try to recall what they were thinking about on their way to the shelter. What did they expect? What did they hope it would be like? Was it a surprise or a disappointment?

This line of questioning did not take us very far. Their answers showed that usually these women had been so emotionally traumatized shortly before they decided to leave home, as well as suffering physical injury in many instances, that what they expected to find in the shelter seemed unimportant at the time. Their thoughts had been narrowly focused on leaving, getting out, *escaping,* and not on what shelter life would be like. The basic urge to survive had become uppermost in their minds. They replied with statements like "I was just so scared of what he was doing to me" or "I was so scared, I can't even remember the ride over here" or "I just knew I had to go. If it wasn't here it would've been someplace else. I couldn't stand it any longer." Women who could recount tales of abuse and victimization calmly would often begin crying as they relived the moment of deciding to leave. Almost none had had any idea of what to expect when they arrived at the shelter except that they and their children would be safe. As several women put it at different times, "I just knew any place was better than where I was."

When a woman does arrive at the shelter there is a routine for admitting her that tries to take the harshness out of bureaucratic procedures. Frequently she is welcomed not only by a counselor but also by other residents. In fact, in the beginning it may not always be clear to her who is a resident and who is a staff worker. Since so many women leave without adequate time to pack or bring necessities for children such as diapers, medication, or extra clothing, providing for their immediate physical needs becomes the first priority.

Depending on how she feels and whatever very obvious problems may need to be dealt with, the staff workers frequently allow the woman two or three days to collect herself before formally interviewing her and assessing her specific problems, needs, and plans for the future. A major part of this task, which is an ongoing activity throughout her stay at the shelter, is to help the woman make her own decisions, sort out her options for the future, choose what seems best for her own situation, and begin taking steps to create a better life for her family, whether or not that includes the batterer.

By this time the battered woman has discovered that she is part of a group living arrangement. At Family Place there are usually 10 or 12 other women and about 15 to 24 children in the same situation as she is. They are at various stages of counseling, reconsidering their lives and goals, and making decisions about what to do. Over the course of weeks they become an extremely important part of her shelter experience. In group discussions or just chatting these women learn to place their own family tragedies in a broader context and to reinterpret their personal victimization (with all its guilt, ambivalence, and embarrassment) as a widespread social problem. They share their pain and unhappiness and lift each other's self-esteem. With the aid of counselors they are encouraged to break out of defeatist or self-destructive moods and think constructively about their own talent and potential.

Adjusting to shelter life can be difficult. Unless they have been to college or a private boarding school where they might have lived in a dormitory, most women are unfamiliar with communal living. They do not always become accustomed easily to the noise of other women's children, the relative lack of privacy, sharing bathrooms, and simply living in close quarters with a dozen other individuals of different ethnic, racial, and educational backgrounds. They also do not always appreciate the fact that every woman is responsible for helping to maintain the shelter by cooking, cleaning, babysitting, and making beds. They literally become part of the maintenance staff. Women who come to Family Place thinking they are becoming residents of an institution where orderlies, nurses, and staff members wait on them are quickly disappointed.

As in any group living situation, there have to be some basic ground rules or agreements on do's and don'ts that benefit all the residents. Some shelters, particularly in the early stages, try to enforce fairly stringent rules and requirements, but this can backfire, making the residents just as dependent and constrained as they were living with domineering men. Other shelters are more lax. Family Place makes clear to each client when she arrives what residents' responsibilities are. As in most other shelters, alcohol, nonprescription drugs, and firearms are absolutely forbidden. So is using any physical violence to discipline a child. (This rule understandably does not please a fair number of women. They complain that the older children exploit the rule and misbehave more when the threat of being slapped or spanked is removed. Violence in any form, however, is the number one taboo in any shelter, and many shelters have been forced to ask women to leave when they refused to honor it.)

Not disclosing the shelter's location is absolutely necessary. Though the police invariably respond as soon as possible if an enraged husband appears at a shelter's door (and they do appear from time to time), the whole concept of a "safe house," which makes a shelter such a relief to residents, rests on the location remaining a secret from the public at large. For this reason Family Place and other shelters will not give directions or a street address over the phone even to a battered woman with a car. Shelter residents' mail must be forwarded to a post office box rather than to any street address. These precautions are necessary. Sisters, mothers, and friends of angry men have been known to call the Hotline, posing as potential residents trying to learn Family Place's address. If the address is discovered, the woman involved will have to be moved elsewhere, usually to another shelter, for her protection as well as that of the other residents. Occasionally a woman has been discovered describing the shelter's location to her boyfriend or husband, perhaps as a way of getting back at him with hints as to where she is or because he plays on her feelings of guilt for leaving him. If this happens, she must leave. Entering a shelter, women are reminded, means adopting a commitment to do something permanent about the violent relationship. Hopping in and out of an abusive relationship, playing games with an abusive man, is unacceptable. And violent men often turn their rage on shelters when they find the women. One only has to see the heavy steel door of Women's Haven, the Fort Worth shelter, with its many dents and knicks from ball peen hammers and rocks, to appreciate the importance of anonymity to shelters.

Women at Family Place have a lenient curfew compared to that of some Texas shelters: 12:00 A.M. on weeknights and 1:00 A.M. on weekends. Residents are adults and have every right to leave the shelter for recreation, to continue their social lives, to keep in touch with life beyond the shelter. They are free to attend movies, to go to bars, to discotheques, or churches. But shelter security requires some accountability from residents. Thus there is a check-in/check-out system that helps prevent a woman from being kidnapped by her spouse and its remaining undiscovered for very long. Women in shelters are not angels, and some try to sabotage this system. Like many shelters, Family Place has an electronically locked door that can only be opened when someone inside trips the current by pressing a loud buzzer. We heard of an incident in one shelter with such an arrangement where several residents deliberately cut the wires to the buzzer so that they could stay out until the early morning and then sneak back in. Needless to say, shelters have enough problems without tolerating women who try to undercut precautions taken for the good of all, and the punishment for such behavior can be expulsion from the shelter.

At first glance many shelters resemble a minimum security prison. But first impressions can be deceiving. In reality, because of the ever-present threat of an infuriated male discovering their locations, many shelters have had to adopt not a prison mentality but rather that of a garrison. Shelters are not places to keep women in but places to keep abusers out. Bars on windows may not be tasteful decor but they, electronic locks, anonymity, and the rule that women must sign in and out when they come and go from shelters help keep shelters what they are first and foremost meant to be: safe places.

Not unexpectedly, some women adjust to shelter life better than others. Some are able to make use of opportunities, and utilize their shelter stay to chart new directions for their lives or resolve the problems causing violence in their homes. Others cannot rise above the daily crises of communal living and thus are probably doomed to re-experience domestic violence when they leave the shelter. Consider the following two examples. The first involves a young woman named Joan who had been at Family Place for about ten days when we talked with her. She reported:

> I have a lot more self-confidence. Before, to pick up the phone and call a friend was nerve-wracking. It sounds weird, I know, but my husband made me stay off the phone just in case he wanted to call me from work. I was told what to wear, the kind of makeup to put on, what to fix for dinner, even who to vote for. Now, for the first time in my life, I put on anything I want to, I read the news section of the paper instead of Ann Landers, and if I screw up at anything, then I am responsible . . . I just know I can make it on my own.

Our other example represents the many petty problems that arise from living in close quarters. Many women are depressed or tense from the strain of living in unfamiliar surroundings and the uncertainty of where they will go after the shelter. Some women are dishonest and steal. Some provoke arguments and direct abusive language at other women. Some almost sociopathically "borrow" clothes, medicine, or small amounts of cash from other women without first asking permission. One shelter worker reported two typical stories about such trivial yet emotionally charged incidents:

May complained that someone, she thought Ann, had slept in her room while she was gone overnight and used almost all of a bag of diapers she'd bought. I told her that I'd tell the regular staff to talk to the others about it. Then, last night about 10:45 Mary came to the volunteer area all agitated, asking me if I knew what was going on. She began to rapidly fill me in on a resident dispute as we walked outside where several other residents were. Jane joined us later. Everyone was pretty worked up, except for Jane who wisely chose to not be involved and suggested everyone go to bed and talk the next day. This was not to be. Apparently, Jane was supervising [baby-sitting] another resident's child and Jane had let the child go play with Mary's children. The resident did not want her child playing with Mary's children and began to verbally abuse Jane and Mary. I think maybe she had been drinking some. I suggested that they avoid each other for the remainder of the night and we could talk out their feelings in group session tomorrow.

But the "bad apples" should not be used as a standard to judge most shelter residents. Shelter life puts burdens on women and children that only complicate the problems they bring with them. Considering crowded living conditions and the constant turnover of shelter residents, we should marvel that conflict is not more usual in shelter life.

AFTER THE SHELTER EXPERIENCE

Most women finally conclude that the shelter experience was worthwhile. The high rate of ex-residents who return to serve as volunteers testifies to the profound change in attitudes that shelters can cause. Family Place staff try to interview each woman before she moves out of the shelter. Some women have lived in the shelter for as long as two months when they review their stay there. In examining the evaluations of Family Place by 262 women, we found that two thirds of them did not have a single negative comment to make about the shelter, the staff, or the services rendered. The relatively few criticisms dealt mainly with adapting to communal living conditions: "I didn't like all the rules and regulations" or "It's hard to get along with some of the residents" or "I can't discipline my children the way I want to." Most women were more positive, however. Asked what was the most useful service of the shelter, one in four mentioned the obvious: It was a safe place to stay. Others cited the reinforcement they received from being with women who shared a common problem. Others benefited specifically from different types of counseling services.

But what happened to them after they left? Did they divorce their husbands? Did they simply return to abusive homes? Or did they return home but somehow manage to handle family violence differently?

The aftermath of a woman's stay in a shelter is one of the most neglected subjects in family violence research. Only recently have shelters begun trying to contact former residents systematically to see what happened to them months and even years after they left. It is not an easy task. In many cases finding the women resembles detective work. Many resume their maiden names, establish independent residences, and for all practical purposes disappear. They become virtually impossible to trace, given the shelter staff's limited time to devote to such a search. Or their friends and employers may protect them, refusing to let callers talk with a woman and offering only to take down the shelter's phone number in case she wants to call back. Some women move out of the community, leaving no forwarding address. Others rejoin the abusers and, for many possible reasons, do not wish to bring the subject up again.

The Texas state legislature in House Bill 1334 designated monies specifically to conduct follow-up studies at state-funded shelters. In addition, an average of eight out of ten women who left Family Place gave the shelter permission to contact them some time in the future. During the summer of 1982, therefore, we tried to find as many former Family Place residents as we could to learn what had happened to them after their stay.

The follow-up proved enormously time-consuming and frustrating. Not surprisingly, the more recently a woman had passed through Family Place the easier she was to track down. After several weeks of concentrated effort we managed to locate only 44 women. We found that about half the women had returned to their husbands or boyfriends, while the rest had moved out, severing the abusive relationship. It is important to mention, however, that of those who returned to the previous relationship only one woman reported that the abuse was worse than it had been before. In the remaining cases the abuse had dropped off noticeably or stopped altogether.

Though the numbers are small, this finding is highly suggestive. It points to the impact a woman's stay in a shelter can have on a violent relationship. Before she came to the shelter the violent man had been able to control the woman and their children, keeping them dependent on him because they believed they had nowhere else to go and no one else to turn to. The shelter experience destroyed that myth, however. After these women returned, their men had to confront the fact that there was someplace the women could go, and that they had left and could leave again if need be. Many women also returned with heightened self-esteem, new skills to deal with male aggression, and a new awareness that made battering unacceptable. How many ultimatums were made by these women to their spouses and lovers is not known. However, it seems probable that a number of men had to think seriously about how they dealt with their wives and common-law mates and try for the first time to develop ways by which they could effectively control their anger.

In addition, the Texas Department of Human Resources collected statistics like ours from every funded shelter in the state, giving a much more conclusive picture of women after they left shelters. It found:

- One fifth of the women returned to the shelter or moved in with friends or relatives.
- One third of the women decided to live independently.

- Half the women returned to live with their spouse or lover.
- Within this half, two thirds said violence had not recurred in the home. When it did recur it was both less frequent and less severe than it had been before the women went to the shelters.

What is more, 71 percent of the women said they felt they had more control over their lives since their stay at the shelter, and 79 percent indicated that the batterer had been or was then in counseling.[7]

This is strong evidence of a positive effect of shelters that until now has not received much attention. It should be noted by critics of shelters who portray them as places that promote divorce. By giving an abused woman a way out of a violent domestic relationship, shelters become a means she can use to pressure the abuser to change. In many cases we can see that the men do improve, either through getting professional help or on their own. Shelters can offer no miracle that will keep violent homes together, for even nonviolent marriages today are subject to tremendous pressures that will break up one out of every two homes. But the case can be made that far from being promoters of divorce, shelters have the opposite effect. They offer battered women alternatives to enduring violence, and that fact alone can modify or eliminate violence altogether in the home. In that sense, shelters can be said to serve the entire family, including the abusive man who is barred from entering them.

THE SPREADING SHELTER MOVEMENT

There are other stories we could have told. The founding of Friends of the Family, the other major shelter in our study, has its own saga and heroic figures. Like Family Place, it began with a grass-roots mandate, a shoestring budget, and the dedication of some hardworking people. Today Friends of the Family is located in a comfortable old two-story house adjacent to a university campus in Denton, Texas, but it began in a squat, rundown one-story house in a deteriorating neighborhood. Its director, Fran Denis, has faced many of the obstacles that her Dallas colleagues overcame and more, for Friends of the Family serves a more rural population. Rural populations are more spread out and public transportation is often nonexistent; conservative attitudes about the family and the man as patriarch tend to be more prevalent; and social service funds can be scarcer. As Karen Mountain, a registered nurse in charge of conducting workshops for rural Texas health professionals on domestic violence, has written:

> Domestic violence is a serious, yet neglected, mental health problem in rural Texas. Complicating this is the scarcity of rural health-care manpower and the lack of rural health providers who are skilled in the delivery of health services to victims of domestic violence.[8]

But space is limited, and we think we have made our point by looking closely at just one shelter. Meanwhile, the shelter movement is spreading, for good reasons. One is sheer demand for shelter services. There are never enough shelters, and they are never large enough to accommodate all the women who seek help. Another reason is their effectiveness. Usually this effectiveness is thought of simply as providing battered family members with temporary nonviolent housing and helping them decide what their future courses should be. Here, however, we have seen another type of effectiveness, and it is long-range. Shelters can actually save families that would otherwise fall apart. They can do more than merely cope with family violence by harboring its victims. They are a force for positive change, and in many instances hold families together. In our society, with all its problems, that is a major achievement.

7

FROM INSULT TO INJURY: THE DEAD ENDS AND POSSIBILITIES OF THE LAW

The American legal system is currently a dead end or a tremendous runaround for most battered women. To believe anything else would be naive. Most public officials, from local police to district attorneys to judges to state legislators to congressmen and women, deny that family violence is a major problem. Or they feel they cannot do much about it. Or they simply wish that its victims would go away. Some take the position that the home is sacrosanct, no matter what happens between family members. They are like the Fort Worth citizens who watched a mugger on a street corner knock a woman to the ground with his fist, then drag her into an alley where he raped her. As she screamed for help he smiled at passers-by and said calmly, "It's all right, she's my wife." No one interfered.[1]

Not all public authorities are ill-informed or unconcerned about family violence, of course, but as sociologists we deal more with trends than with exceptions. In this chapter we will look at different levels of the legal system and how each handles the domestic violence problem. As we will show, there are frustrations on all sides, both for the woman trying to find help and for the people who logically should help her. Many of our comments about officials' handling of domestic violence complaints will be negative, but there is hope. There are positive, workable ways to improve the situation. They have been tried or are being tried in such states as Texas and California and there is no reason they cannot be used elsewhere. Before discussing improvements, however, we will examine the realities of the legal system as it is.

THE LAW AND WHY IT DOESN'T WORK

Many people, when they hear horror stories about battered women and children, have a naive reaction such as "Won't the police take care of that?" or "Doesn't the state have agencies to monitor it?" or "Don't we have laws for things like that?"

In truth, neither the police nor the state can do nearly enough to alleviate the problem of family violence. This is, sadly, not surprising, given that in America abuse of a woman is traditionally considered a man's right or at least their private affair, just as violent discipline of a child has been seen as the prerogative of the head of a household. Moreover, family violence has long been considered a civil rather than a criminal matter. As a result of our society's traditional acceptance of a man's right to give his wife "discipline," battered women are not afforded equality in the eyes of the law. It was as recently as 1977 that the Washington State Supreme Court reversed the murder conviction of a woman after taking under advisement the impact of a "long and unfortunate history of sex discrimination" on the plea of self-defense. This specific case (*The State of Washington* v. *Wanrow*, 88 Washington, 2nd 548, 1977) represents the most direct statement of a theory of self-defense for battered women adopted by an appellate court. In the Wanrow trial the judge had advised the jury that a lethal weapon was not permitted in self-defense unless one party being assaulted had reasonable grounds to believe that he or she was in imminent danger of death or great bodily harm. Considerably smaller than the abusing man and already crippled by a bone-breaking injury, the wife had nevertheless been convicted of murdering him when he attacked her. The Washington Supreme Court, in overturning the verdict, ruled:

> [The judge's instruction] leaves the jury with the impression that the objective standard to be applied is that applicable to an altercation between two men. The impression created — that a 5 foot 4 inch woman with a cast on her leg and using a crutch must, under the law, somehow repel an assault by a 6 foot 2 inch intoxicated man without employing weapons in her defense—violates the respondent's right to equal protection of the law.

That the woman's justified self-defense even in this exaggerated situation had to be decided by a state supreme court is an illustration of how insensitive the entire legal system can be to domestic violence. In the state of Texas it was 1968 before there was legislation passed making even assault of *any* person, man or woman, outside the family a criminal offense. With the exception of laws concerning child abuse, there are few statutes in the nation that protect people against people if the attacker happens to be a family member. The concept of assault in the criminal sense is practically unheard-of as far as family violence is concerned. The frequent dead ends that the legal system creates for abused women trying to get help and find justice raises the suspicion that authorities such as the police, judges, and district attorneys may not want to be reminded that many American families are not the idyllic, loving, caring units portrayed in Norman Rockwell's paintings, or that they view the family as so sacred that almost nothing that goes on within it could justify intervention.

A good example of the law's reluctance to protect family members who are abused is the recently passed House Bill 1743 in the state of Texas. Intended as a measure to get women better police response by allowing the police to arrest a violent man without a warrant, it states explicitly that a policeman may arrest "persons who the peace officer has probable cause to believe have committed an assault resulting in bodily injury to another person and [when] the peace officer has probable cause to believe that there is immediate danger of further bodily injury to that person." This law thus allows the peace officer to make a warrantless arrest if in his judgment future assault is imminent. It should have resulted in more arrests of batterers. But did it?

We spoke with one Dallas judge who helped write the law, and he was obviously proud that he had helped provide the police with a way to deal better with domestic violence incidents. In reality, however, peace officers are very reluctant to use this law. A careful reading of the law shows that it requires a policeman to be a soothsayer, predicting that the wife will be in future danger. When the police arrive the situation may have changed. The man may have cooled off, the woman is no longer hysterical, the children have stopped screaming. The man tells the police: "I lost my temper but I'm okay now" or "I had a little too much to drink, but I've sobered up" or "I'm sorry this happened, but we always argue with a lot of noise." There is no obvious assault in progress, and perhaps no sign of violence. The police have no wish to prolong the call. Hence there is no arrest.

In a recent publication entitled "Responding to Spouse Abuse and Wife Beating: A Guide for Police," the following description of the police perspective appeared:

> The officers were asked about which factors they consider to be important in their decisions whether to arrest. They responded that an arrest is likely if the following are present: commission of a felony, serious injury to the victim, use of a weapon, and use of violence against police officers. When deciding not to arrest, officers assign the most importance to the following: refusal of the victim to press charges, victims' tendency to drop charges, lack of serious injury, and an intoxicated victim or assailant.

It went on to note sources of police frustration in the domestic violence situation:

> Many of the officers surveyed expressed frustration, disdain, and feelings of inadequacy about their role in these cases. Some of these feelings they attributed to poor training, a lack of clear agency policy and procedural directives, and a lack of incentive to spend time handling and following up on spousal violence calls. Additional factors were statutory constraints, especially those limiting arrest authority in misdemeanor assault cases; the refusal of the criminal justice system to accept and process these cases; and stress and indifference resulting from overexposure to interpersonal conflict and violence.[2]

This study was conducted by the Police Executive Research Forum in Washington, D.C., and not by outsiders unsympathetic to the problems of police officers. Thus, its conclusions can be taken as accurately reflecting the feelings and sentiments of the police regarding family violence. As our study will show, many women sense these feelings on the part of police, and frequently this awareness contributes to their unwillingness to ask the police for help. An enormous proportion of battered women simply never call the police. Or if they do call, the lack of meaningful assistance discourages them and they rarely call again. More shocking is the fact that the police many times do not even respond to domestic disturbance calls, particularly if the caller is someone known to have called several times before.

These are strong indictments of the legal system and persons responsible for administering justice. Let us now consider them in more detail.

LEGISLATORS

Lawmakers rank high in ignorance and unconcern over domestic violence. Perhaps it is because they have to deal with it so rarely, at least in discharging their professional duties. A revealing example of this could be seen when H.R. 2977, the Act to Prevent Domestic Violence, was debated by Congress in the autumn of 1980. The bill would have appropriated $15 million to help set up programs to combat domestic violence run and designed by states and local communities. States would have had to put up matching funds, and no individual project would have received more than $50,000. The highest priority among such projects was to establish "safe houses," or shelters, for victims of family violence.

There was the usual flurry of misunderstanding about what shelters are and therefore what the impact of this legislation would be on the family. It is said that one congressman thought that domestic violence involved terrorism at airports! However, the bill was really halted by conservative opposition. At hearings before a conference committee (attended scrupulously by "pro-family" Moral Majority advocates who opposed the bill), Senator Garlan Humphrey of New Hampshire claimed that shelters for battered women would actually be anti-family "indoctrination centers." And ultra-conservative Senator Jesse Helms of North Carolina claimed that shelters would promote the "disintegration of the family." As nationally syndicated columnist Ellen Goodman wryly noted shortly before the bill died in committee:

> Apparently an intact family with a broken wife is better than a broken family with an intact ex-wife . . . According to these fantasies, the woman who heads for a shelter is the one responsible for breaking up the family, not the husband who beat her. The shelters are dangerous precisely because they might suggest that her husband had no right to "enforce his authority" with a left hook to the jaw.[3]

There is a particular irony in such sentiments coming out of Washington, since the nation's capital is no stranger to wife abuse. One year before the Act to Prevent Domestic Violence was allowed to die, a House subcommittee held hearings to consider legislation that would appropriate $65 million in grants over a three-year period to family violence shelters. Dr.

Saul Edelstein, head of emergency services at George Washington University Hospital, testified that the wives of prominent men in Washington were unlikely to report officially any beatings their husbands gave them. But, as Dr. Edelstein reported:

> ... wives of congressmen will admit [being beaten] to the nurses, but they don't want that on their charts ... Battered wives in Washington refuse to report their husbands because the publicity could ruin their spouses' careers, cutting back their own source of income ...

Dr. Edelstein told reporters that George Washington University Hospital regularly treated wives who had been beaten by high-ranking Washington officials.[4]

Nor are state legislatures centers of sympathetic understanding for the domestic violence problem. In our own state of Texas we have seen some legislators respond to attempts to find some permanent funding base for shelters with incredible displays of sexist derision, flippancy, and blaming-the-victim mentality. For example, when state senator Chet Brooks introduced a bill to use 4 percent of the revenues raised by a mixed drink tax to help support shelters, witnesses came forward at public hearings before the Senate Committee on Human Resources to testify for or against it. After giving her testimony in favor of the tax, Debby Tucker (representing the Texas Council on Family Violence) was questioned by Senator John Leedom:

> What about the wife going back to mother, or some other member of the family? ... One of the checks you used to have on an abusive son-in-law was a father. My concern is that you [battered wives' shelters] are helping to change that. The pro-family concept is that the family circle is not just the husband and wife, it's children and aunts and uncles, brothers and sisters ... Why can't we aim that troubled person into a loving environment?[5]

This is a typical complaint against shelters (that they undermine the family and men's authority), which shows a total lack of understanding of what shelters do, the real problems they confront, the link between a current batterer and his violent father, and facile lip-service to some illusory "pro-family" position supposedly opposed by shelters. This is by no means a position peculiar to Texas. In 1977 in New Hampshire, for instance, the state's Commission on the Status of Women voted 9 to 1 against a program to help victims of wife-battering. "You can't legislate love in the home," said one female commissioner. Another commission member (also a woman) put the real prejudices of the commission very clearly: "Some women's libbers irritate the hell out of their husbands." [6]

The image of shelters as threats to the family, filled with misfit feminists whose marital problems stem from the women's liberation movement, is contradicted by the facts. (Never mind the children. Most legislators are totally unaware that large numbers of children, many of them also battered, are served by shelters.) As we showed in Chapter two, shelters tend to be filled with women who are the exact opposite of the radical feminist stereotype. They are predominantly young homemakers and mothers without jobs, who are living traditional female lives. And as Chapter six demonstrated, shelters frequently *reunite* families—families often change for the better and become nonviolent because of shelters.

Thus the dominant legislative response to domestic violence is either apathy or, worse, traditional prejudice. Under these circumstances it is not surprising that fewer than 15 states have enacted legislation providing funding for shelters for battered women and children, and most of this funding is not on any permanent or long-term basis.[7] Nor is it a surprise that many states have no civil remedies, shelter services, statistical monitoring of domestic violence, relevant police training, or criminal statutes or proceedings regarding domestic violence whatsoever. These include Alabama, Arizona, Georgia, Idaho, Mississippi, Oklahoma, South Dakota, and Wyoming. Other states have absolutely no statutes concerned with wife-beating, making it virtually impossible to bring charges against an assailant if he has any form of an intimate relationship with a woman (Colorado, Connecticut, Delaware, Illinois, Kentucky, Louisiana, Maryland, New Jersey, South Carolina, Virginia, and West Virginia).

One has only to sit through public hearings on the subject and note how few of the legislators or their staff members even take the trouble to attend, to realize the low priority given so far to the growing epidemic of domestic violence. This is no doubt the reason that the federal Office of Domestic Violence closed its doors in April 1981. Established in the spring of 1979, the ODV was the only federal agency making an attempt to monitor domestic violence on a national scale.

> During 1979 the Office of Domestic Violence focused on dissemination of public information and technical assistance, which included the creation of a national clearinghouse to develop, collect, and disseminate data on domestic violence ... for fiscal year 1980 the Office of Domestic Violence was authorized $1.2 million in program funds. With this money it focused on technical assistance programs, public awareness activities, and demonstration grants for comprehensive community services.[8]

But apathy killed it. Two years after its creation, the Office of Domestic Violence was nonfunded out of existence by Congress as a low-priority need.

DISTRICT ATTORNEYS

A fact many citizens forget is that the choice to prosecute a nonfederal crime is totally in the hands of the prosecuting attorney in the local district attorney's office. The state, not private individuals, decides whether to prosecute individuals for crimes. What this means to a battered woman is that whether the assault is considered a Class C misdemeanor (minor bruises and lacerations), a Class A misdemeanor (more severe bruises, black eyes, or cuts), or aggravated assault (broken bones, hospitalization necessary), the decision to press criminal charges against a husband or boyfriend is evaluated by a prosecuting attorney who may decline to prosecute the case. The odds are that he (or she) will decide against it. Furthermore, the prosecuting attorney is rarely accountable for such decisions.

District attorneys' offices do not particularly like domestic violence cases. They are impatient with women who become ambivalent about pressing criminal charges against mates for a wide variety of reasons. They are interested in conviction rates, and convictions do not come easily in domestic violence cases. The district attorney is a political creature, and there is no political glamour in prosecuting any except the most sensational domestic violence cases. Many times district attorneys share the general prejudice about such cases—the woman asked for the violence, or enjoys it, or deserves it. "Any woman dumb enough to marry such a jerk deserves what she gets," commented an assistant district attorney in Fort Worth when asked about wife-beating by a reporter. He boasted of encountering hundreds of wife-beating cases each month, apparently approaching each with this attitude.[9]

"The D.A. won't typically prosecute, not until she's been put in the hospital, or is dead," a Fort Worth lawyer who frequently represents battered women told us. "Then they *may* prosecute." In an interview with a local journalist the Fort Worth district attorney's office candidly agreed with this lawyer's cynical assessment:

> "Nine out of ten times we don't file on these cases," one assistant D.A. said. "Because they [the women] usually will tell us to drop it." He said, "A lot of these people are regulars. The only answer often is a divorce." He pointed out that in the last crime statistics report released for Tarrant County, the number of assaults had gone down. "That's because we don't file on them," he said.
>
> He said that even if a case is brought to court, many people in Tarrant County (who make up the juries) think a man has the right to beat up his wife. "So we have to show

that this assault is different from the assaults you see every day. Even broken bones are not good enough. It's good [as evidence for the prosecution] if she gets shot." [10]

In a recent report by the United States Commission on Civil Rights on the domestic violence problem the following seven criticisms were made about district attorneys' offices:

1. Prosecutors enjoy wide discretion to determine which criminal cases will be prosecuted and often accord low priority to cases involving domestic violence.
2. The rate of prosecution and conviction in criminal cases drops sharply when there is a prior or present relationship between the alleged assailant and the victim.
3. Some prosecutors hesitate to file charges against abusers, based on their belief that domestic violence is a noncriminal, personal matter or that prosecution would adversely affect the parties' marriages.
4. Prosecutors often treat victims of spouse abuse as if they, rather than the defendants, were accused of criminal conduct.
5. Prosecutors frequently attribute the low rate of prosecution in spouse abuse cases to lack of victim cooperation, which may become a self-fulfilling prophecy. Prosecutors who believe that abuse victims will not cooperate with the prosecution of their cases frequently discourage the victims from using the criminal justice system.
6. Prosecutors rarely subpoena victims to testify in abuse cases, although such action frequently could circumvent victims' noncooperation.
7. Prosecutors frequently charge spouse abusers with crimes less serious than their conduct seems to warrant.[11]

Our 542 shelter residents were asked if they had contacted their local district attorney's office to inquire about filing assault charges on the abusing men. Most had not. They had not known how to file charges or had been discouraged from doing so. Some women willing to press charges were repeatedly called by the district attorney's office and asked if they were sure they wanted to go through with proceedings. Even the few women who did pursue the matter further were unhappy with the results. The women reported their experiences:

- I didn't know who to contact.
- I had talked to police and other people and they said that they (the district attorney's office) did not do that any more.
- I didn't know I could while I'm still married.
- I haven't had any money to file on him.
- They told me you can't file charges unless you've been to the hospital and have proof that he can hurt you all he wants.
- No, I didn't. The police told me they would handle it.

However, these stories pale beside the advice a Southfield, Michigan, district attorney gave one battered woman in a memorandum. Recall our brief synopsis of *The Burning Bed* that began Chapter one. Then consider the following:

A mother of two who sought relief from her husband's beatings said Tuesday she cried quite a bit over a city attorney's memorandum suggesting that she get matches and gasoline and contact Francine Hughes.

The Francine Hughes mentioned in the memo was acquitted in Lansing in November of murdering her husband by reason of insanity. Mrs. Hughes said her husband had abused her for years and admitted pouring gasoline around his bed as he slept and setting it aflame.

"I was hurt and embarrassed," said Dorothy Ann Nelson, who had sought help from the police and was sent a copy of the memo written by a city government attorney.

Assistant City Attorney Richard Miller said he wrote the memo after deciding he did not have enough evidence to seek a warrant against Mrs. Nelson's husband.[12]

There are many reasons that district attorneys handle domestic violence cases so reluctantly. As we've seen, many women initiate charges against men but the men then promise to reform, play on their sympathies, or remind the women of their economic dependence. What will she do if he is put away and cannot work? Or the evidence is not conclusive from the prose-cutor's viewpoint. Why has she put up with the abuse for so long? Why didn't she leave before? Many district attorneys look on family violence as a civil rather than a criminal matter. As a result, estimates of how many battering men are ever prose-cuted reach as low as 2 percent.[13]

As we shall indicate shortly, however, the district attorney can be effective in stopping the runaround that battered women often encounter. And we do not mean to portray all district attorneys as callous about domestic violence. We close this sec-tion with an example of the district attorney's point of view. A former assistant district attorney in Dallas, who shared her frustrations and experiences with us, alerted us to an occasion when she objected to columnist Ann Landers' advice on family violence. In doing so she gave an articulate summary of the problems such officials have in coping with domestic violence. Ann Landers had received the following letter:

Dear Ann Landers:

I was seeing a 48-year-old man on a steady basis. I am a young-looking 39. Last December a 17-year-old girl moved into Rodney's apartment. I thought nothing of it when he said she was a friend of his 20-year-old niece. The arrange-ment was that she would pay half the rent, a good deal for them both, seeing as how she was new in town, needed a place to live and couldn't afford an apartment alone. A friend tipped me off that the 17-year-old was no friend of anybody's and that she and Rodney were shacked up. When I confronted him, he slapped me around, loosened three side teeth, and gave me a shiner. The following day I laid an assault charge on him. The charge got an unusual amount of publicity, and Rodney is now in danger of los-ing his job. Also, his ex-wife has threatened to take away his visiting privileges (they have three underage children). The question: should I drop charges or not, Ann? I can't handle this kind of guilt and I am

—Very Mixed Up in Ohio

Ann Landers' reply was:

Dear Very Mixed:

Drop the charges *and* Rodney. (P.S. There's an awful lot
of sound advice in that 5-word answer. I hope you take it.)[14]

The former assistant district attorney, outraged by Ann
Landers' advice, sent the following letter:

August 10, 1982

Ms. Ann Landers
Post Office Box 11995
Chicago, Illinois 60611

Re: Response to "Very Mixed Up in Ohio"
     Column in Dallas (Texas) *Morning News*:
     August 6, 1982

Dear Ms. Landers:

"Very Mixed Up in Ohio" had been beaten by Rodney
when she confronted him about his relationship with another woman. You advised her to "Drop the charges and
Rodney."
   For four years I was the Assistant Criminal District Attorney in Dallas County, Texas, assigned to the Civilian
Complaint Desk. My duties were to answer inquiries and
file criminal charges brought to our attention by members
of the public, as distinguished from those initiated by the
police or other peace officers. A significant percentage of the
matters brought to my attention concerned women who had
been beaten by men.
   Many friends in law enforcement and counseling join me
in considering your advice to your correspondent to be
wrong. Under no circumstances should "Very Mixed Up"
have tried to drop the charges against Rodney.
   The main difficulty faced by "battered women" has for
years been that they could get no help from law enforce-

ment agencies. The standard rebuttal from the police and from state's attorneys' offices has been that too many victims refuse to follow through when charges are filed.

A victim all too often does not follow through because (1) she is blackmailed into believing she will suffer even more horrible attacks from the assailant if she persists or (2) she fears economic consequences if her breadwinner is fined or incarcerated or (3) her guilt-reaction or the "sweet talk" of the assailant persuades her "he didn't mean to do it" and "he'll never do it again." I know from following your columns for many years that you are aware of this.

If an assailant receives no criticisms, no sanctions, and no punishments for his first attack, he knows that he can get away with violence. The first time he may simply hurt the victim a little, but the attacks usually escalate into severe injuries and even killing. Society by its silence has condoned this.

Victims have felt helpless because the police would not become involved in "domestic disputes." The police's non-action was occasioned by the District Attorney's Office's refusal to prosecute. The District Attorney's reluctance was based on too many victims refusing to follow through and testify against their assailants. To put it another way, the District Attorney would not back up the police who would not back up the victims who would not back up the District Attorney. I saw this vicious cycle in Dallas.

Had "Very Mixed Up" come to me at the District Attorney's Office asking to drop charges against Rodney, I would have replied, "No way!" I would point out to her that the State, not an individual, prosecutes crimes. She can then respond to Rodney's importunities or threats that she's tried to get the charges dropped but the so-and-so at the D.A.'s office would not let her. For her fear and guilt feelings, I would suggest she get in touch with a counseling service.

As for Rodney, I might recommend that he get a fine or serve some time in jail, but in any event would have the judge, as a part of Rodney's sentence, require that he receive counseling about his violent propensities. I cannot be sympathetic to Rodney about the prospect of losing his job or losing visiting privileges with his children. A conventional method of punishment for assailants is a term in jail. Rodney knew he risked that when he slugged "Very Mixed

Up." If I were Rodney's ex-wife, I would be leery about his being with the children if I thought he were prone to violence. (Since she was his *ex*-wife, I doubt she was very surprised at what happened to "Very Mixed Up." It's likely she, too, had been in your correspondent's condition.)

The fact that the criminal charges were filed against Rodney shows that Ohio authorities were prepared to assist "Very Mixed Up." Telling her to drop the charges enforces the vicious cycle of nonaction. It negates the efforts of many law enforcement and counseling agencies to send forth the message that such violence is not condoned and will not be tolerated. I know from your columns that you know this. My friends in police departments, the Dispute Mediation Service, the Pastoral Counseling Center and the Domestic Violence Intervention Alliance join me in a plea to you to retract your advice. You often deplore the violence of our society. We beg that you not block the efforts of those with the power and desire to extinguish some of that violence.

Yours very truly,

Mary Neal Sisk[15]

The D.A. had made her point. Two months later Ann Landers replied in her column:

Dear Readers:

Get out the cat-o'-nine-tails, a wet noodle won't do. I told "Mixed Up in Ohio" to "Drop the charges *and* Rodney." (He loosened her bridgework.) I should have advised, "Drop Rodney and by all means press charges. No man should get away with beating up on a woman." [16]

JUDGES

It has been estimated that if a woman has been physically abused and wishes to press charges against the abuser the odds of her case ever reaching a courtroom are no better than 100 to 1. But even if the case makes it to trial, the question of what to do with domestic violence cases remains. Part of this problem rests with judges.

Judges often have an unclear idea of where domestic assault falls legally. In states where battered women's complaints could be considered by either family or criminal courts, judges have frequently referred most cases to family courts. The power of a judge to define a case as criminal assault as opposed to a civil suit is critical, and in many instances judges simply treat such cases as family squabbles not worth serious criminal proceedings. In the opinion of one expert:

> Judges sitting in criminal courts display the same prejudices as police and prosecutors, even though they see battered wives who have refused to be discouraged and have cooperated with the prosecution. Statistics . . . show that there are few prosecutions resulting from thousands of requests for warrants. This may indicate that only the most serious cases, in which the victim believes that jail is the only way to stop her husband's attacks and the prosecutor believes he has sufficient evidence for conviction, go to trial. Yet the judges treat these cases as though there had been no attempts to screen them out on the police and prosecutor level. They tell women to forget the injuries and reconcile with their husbands. Marriage counseling is ordered without consideration of the seriousness of the assault, or women are told to get a divorce and the case is dismissed.[17]

This attitude on the part of many judges is also reflected in the relatively light sentences they give those few men convicted of beating up their spouses. Certainly the sentences are much lighter than if someone outside the home had been assaulted by the man. This was one specific criticism made by the U.S. Commission on Civil Rights in reviewing how the legal system handles domestic violence. Judges tend to be lenient not just with abusers who are convicted but also when these men violate restraining orders during divorces and ignore peace bonds. Abusive men are given "second chances," so that temporary restraining orders and other legal protections for abused women become meaningless. The inescapable conclusion is that many judges simply do not see domestic violence as an important enough problem to consider beyond individual cases. Not only do the majority of domestic assault cases never reach a court-room or judge, but when such cases do come before judges, in the words of the commission, "Many judges approach abuse cases as isolated incidents of aberrant behavior between con-senting adults rather than as examples of widespread societal problems." [18]

Even more maddening to advocates for the rights of abused women are instances where judges seemingly go out of their way to let off serious abusers, even murderers, with the lightest sentences possible. For example, in two recent sensational mur-der trials, which received a good deal of media coverage, the judges played critical roles in greatly reducing the punishment of convicted woman-abusers.

In Oakland, California, a newly appointed Alameda Superior Court judge named Henry Ramsey ended his first homicide trial by reducing a jury's conviction of second-degree murder to manslaughter. He did it claiming he was exercising his au-thority as the "thirteenth juror" in the trial. The defendant, 33-year-old Jimmy Springer, had stabbed his girlfriend three times, killing her. Some months before the murder, he had broken her arm, choked her, and threatened to kill her. Evi-dence during the trial had shown Springer to be excessively jealous of his girlfriend, a classic abusive male. Judge Ramsey justified the reduced sentence on the grounds that he had "rea-sonable doubts" that Springer really intended to kill the woman. He felt that Springer had acted in the heat of passion, referring to Springer's considerable jealousy. The verdict out-raged the prosecutor, horrified the courtroom audience and the victim's family, and even drew protest from the jury. But prose-cutors, unlike defense attorneys, have no opportunity for ap-pealing verdicts. They have only one chance. There was no way to reverse the decision.

A second example occurred recently in San Antonio, Texas.

There Judge Preston Dial pronounced a relatively light ten-year prison sentence on a man convicted of the murder of his wife and voluntary manslaughter of his father-in-law. These were, in the prosecutor's words, "execution-style slayings." One night in the fall of 1980 defendant Francisco Javier Mendez put a gun to the temple of his sleeping 15-year-old pregnant wife and fired two bullets into her brain. Afterward he scrawled "Frankie Loves Sylvia" across her chest with a red grease pencil. Ballistic experts estimated that he killed his father-in-law in the same way, firing into him from a distance of only a few inches as he slept. The exasperated assistant district attorney who prosecuted the case took little satisfaction in winning it. As he pointed out to journalists, the defendant would be eligible for parole in less than two years.

What is shown by these examples as well as numerous studies by legal experts is judges' low level of awareness of the realities of family violence. Judges are well schooled in legal procedures and rules of admissible evidence during trials, but the average judge is uninformed about domestic violence as a social problem, not just that of a specific family. Better understanding of the problem could influence how judges sentence convicted batterers, how they try cases of assault of abused women, and how they might institute alternative, innovative ways to combat family violence from their position on the bench. As it is, the judge who takes the more informed, positive stance toward family violence that we are advocating is an exception. Even in Austin, Texas, a city that has an innovative program to give convicted battering men the opportunity to enter anger-management therapy in lieu of gaining a criminal record, only one out of five municipal judges is willing to suggest this option. The others continue using the same tired, ineffectual method for coping with family violence, treating such violence as if, short of murder, it is qualitatively different from ordinary assault; regarding the abused women as complainers or inadequate wives; and perceiving the whole problem as limited to a relatively small number of problem families. As long as judges continue to see each domestic violence case as an unfortunate individual instance, and not as simply one example of a spreading larger problem, they will continue to process what few domestic violence cases they ever see to the satisfaction of nobody.

THE POLICE

The police are the most immediate resource many women think of when they become fearful of violence in their homes. In many instances, therefore, the police confront the family violence problem even before shelter workers do. They are, after all, agents for keeping the peace, and family violence is certainly a breach of that peace. The irony is that most of the time, when such violence occurs the police are not called. In our study we found that only one in ten women involved in a domestic violence situation actually called the police for help. Other research, conducted by Dr. Raymond H.C. Teske, Jr., at the Criminal Justice Center at Sam Houston State University in Huntsville, Texas, showed that throughout the state only one out of five female victims called the police.[19]

But at the same time virtually every police department of any size in the country feels it is swamped with domestic disturbance calls. Legal expert Raymond I. Parnas reported that the everyday police response to the minor family conflict probably exceeds the total number of murders, aggravated batteries, and all other serious crimes.[20] In the city of Chicago, for example, Parnas found that one third of the noncriminal calls to police involve family violence, and these calls make up 83 percent of all calls to police. The situation is similar in the Dallas–Fort Worth metropolitan area and in other large Texas cities.

Yet seldom do the police resolve the violence problem to everyone's satisfaction, least of all their own, when they answer such calls. Most police responses to domestic disturbances rarely result in anyone being arrested. They do not and cannot get at the causes of the violence. They usually do not and cannot prevent future violence from occurring. They are blamed by shelter workers, shelter movement sympathizers, and the battered women for letting the abuser get away with violence. Worst of all, they put themselves in a hopeless situation which can threaten their own lives.

The role of the police in family violence is a frustrating one for all concerned, but it is worth taking a look at the factors influencing why the police respond the way they do when called by battered women, if only to present a realistic picture of what help such women can expect. We will then also have a better understanding of how the police could be better used by the entire legal system to create a more effective way of handling family violence.

Danger

Police are adamant when they say that domestic disturbances are among the most dangerous situations they face. A spokesman for the Fort Worth police department claimed that such calls for help "take their toll in policemen's lives. We have a great many officers killed in answering these calls." [21] The Texas Department of Human Resources found the same general opinion in a survey it conducted among the chiefs of police and patrolmen of thirteen law enforcement units in the state:

> The officers feel that domestic violence calls are the most dangerous type of call. More injuries are sustained in response to this type of call than to any other... The officers are usually called to the scene after the incident has become a crisis situation. He is the first person there in any official capacity and is charged with bringing control to the situation... Injuries sustained by officers responding to domestic disturbance calls range from scratches and bruises to hospitalization with broken bones and gunshot wounds. The most frequent injuries are the result of an assailant's hands, feet or teeth. Firearms and knives are used to a much lesser degree. Every officer interviewed had suffered various injuries on more than one occasion.[22]

The FBI's yearly Uniform Crime Reports also repeatedly show that an average of one third of reported assaults on police officers occur in connection with domestic disturbance calls.

What makes family violence so dangerous for police? The most important element is the uncertainty factor. The violent family is a totally unpredictable situation. The domestic quarrel may be only a mild spat where the abuse is limited to profanity, or it may involve lethal weapons; it may begin as one and quickly escalate into the other. There is no way to tell. Additionally, the sight of police entering a home or trying to arrest a violent man can suddenly transform the beleaguered, battered woman who tearfully called them into an ardent defender of her husband. This transformation can be abrupt and uncanny, as policemen who have been suddenly bitten, kicked, stabbed, and leapt upon when their backs were turned to battered women can testify. Unpredictable situations understandably create tension, and they may turn into life-threatening scenes that explain the reluctance on the part of police to become involved.

Another reason domestic violence is such a dangerous problem for police to mediate is the emotion involved. To many batterers (and their victims) the boundaries of homes are sacred. In their eyes the police can appear to be illegitimate, uninvited invaders, regardless of whether family members called them or not. The passion to resist them can be intense, increasing the odds of serious violence.

Police claims of the volatile emotions that often erupt into violence rechanneled at them are too reliable and numerous to be dismissed as mere exaggeration or imagination. For police, physical danger is a constant occupational hazard, and they, better than anybody, learn where to expect it most often.

Crying Wolf

In the opinion of many police officers they are being asked to sort out, resolve, and otherwise manage the ordinary marital problems of far too many couples. That, they feel, is not their job. According to them, a large proportion of women call for police assistance when they really are crying out for marriage counselors. They may indicate over the telephone that they are in imminent physical danger, but they are really "crying wolf," hoping that this time the abusive man will be intimidated by the police presence into stopping his violence. Thus, when they call police stations repeatedly these women develop reputations among police radio dispatchers, desk sergeants, and squad patrols that lower the odds of their pleas for help being taken very seriously in the future. If they call and the police respond, but they are then unwilling to press assault charges against the abusive man, they risk becoming regarded as time-consuming crank callers and being placed far down on the list of important responses.

Experienced police we talked with held an almost contemptuous view of marginally violent couples who required police intervention:

> I approach it as if I am about to counsel a couple of children who have been in a play-school fight. Generally the reasons for their fighting are certainly juvenile, such as the fact that the husband stayed out a half hour later than he told his wife. There is an attitude on my part not to be really violent. I don't think that my tendency is to really swell up and grab my shotgun and put my helmet on and expect that I'm about to go into a full-grown battle. I think that my tendency is to really believe that I'm about to run across a couple of people who have gotten to a point of view in life which is really almost on a juvenile scale, and they need a referee.

> In almost fourteen years of being a policeman I have handled a few that have involved stabbings and shootings or shots fired and things like that, but in the vast majority of them the thing that they're arguing about, no matter who started it, is really petty. Usually it is a lot of "I'm going to call the police on you and get you in trouble." And when we get there it is more spite than anything else. One will scream about what a rotten son of a bitch this guy is and tell all the horrible things ... and about half-way through

it the other says, "Now wait a minute, you think that's bad? Listen to this!" And he proceeds to tell me all the horrible things about his wife that I'm supposed to get mad at. It is one trying to impress us as to how rotten the other one is. We just have to get them separated and calm them down and let them know that we're not going to take sides. I just feel like here's a couple of people who are probably about half drunk and have decided that they want to call the police and get the other one in trouble, and the vast majority of times it can be settled. There really is no crime, and there hasn't been any type of assault. You just have to negotiate with these two people to get their heads back where they should be.

We had a woman in town a couple of years ago who had called the station up to eight or nine times a night, and when we wouldn't satisfy her she would call the county sheriff's office or she would call the state police, the city police, the fire department, and places like that. She would wait until the husband was asleep and then call us and say her husband had been beating her up and that he was drunk. Of course we would get there and wake him up and find out there was absolutely no basis for a crime—not just because it was worthless but because there were no other facts to support her contention! She would be sitting there in her house and everything would be fine and nothing would be disturbed in the house ... There was no indication that any kind of crime had occurred other than that she said her husband had slapped her and that he had been pretending to be asleep. We would just say, "Well, goodnight, he's asleep and he's not going to bother you anymore." Ten minutes later we would get a call from the sheriff's office that she had called them and said the local police wouldn't do anything. So she wanted them to come out. Pretty soon we would get a call from the state police saying they had a call from a woman that was being abused by her husband and would we follow up on the disturbance. You know, she was finally committed to a mental institution.

Police receive a large number of such calls and usually resent them as nuisances. The abuse in many cases is minimal, and it

certainly does not warrant arrests on criminal charges. And, as
the police have reminded us, each time a police car answers any
disturbance call, domestic or otherwise, it can easily cost taxpayers at least one hundred dollars or more. Many police officers see the run-of-the-mill domestic disturbance, dangerous as
it may be potentially to them, as no more serious than a cat
stuck in a tree is to a firefighter.

Lack of Power

Most people have unrealistic expectations of the police. Perhaps this may be blamed on television, where the average patrolman routinely solves crimes and where cops, like the surgeons on doctor shows, become intimately involved in citizens'
personal problems. One policeman summarized the problem
for us by saying, "I think the people have a real misconception
of what the role of police is in the civil disturbance." There is
a tendency for battered women to think, at least the first time,
that they can simply call the police and have the violent man
taken away. But the police can only make an arrest when they
actually witness the violence or if evidence of past violence is
indisputable, as when there is blood, an open wound, or severe
injury.

In reviewing thousands of Hotline calls to Dallas's Family
Place we found that the police had arrested a total of only 20
of these batterers. These arrests only occurred when the man
beat or struck his wife in the presence of officers, or when he
became violent or abusive toward them. In one case the man
threw a punch at his wife, she ducked, and he hit a policeman
standing next to her. In several others the men were still threatening the women with weapons when the police arrived and
refused to put the guns or knives down as ordered. Several men
were drunk and verbally abusive to the police, and after following them out to the squad cars with strings of profanities were
arrested for public intoxication or disorderly conduct.

Incredibly, on several occasions the *victims* of violence were
arrested. In one Dallas house to which police were called they

learned that the battered woman had a number of outstanding traffic and parking tickets, so they took her away under arrest. In another case a woman's husband chased her out of the house late at night, waving a machete in the air. Clad only in her nightgown, she manged to flag down a passing police car (while the husband hid) and was arrested for hitchhiking! One other woman became so enraged at her husband when he told police that he had never battered her that she tried to slap him, he stepped aside, and she mistakenly clipped the officer.

Often there is violence by both parties, and if the woman loses she expects the police to support her. Said one police officer we interviewed:

> She demands that you arrest the husband because she called the police. However, when you get into this situation and you start finding out the facts you find out that in fact he slapped her but she attacked him with a butcher knife. And when you talk about criminal offenses very often the person who calls the police looking for our protection is really the one who committed the more serious criminal offense. I think that is a very important factor, considering a lot of these people, just because they are the ones who picked up the phone and said, "I need a police officer." They expect that we are on their side automatically when we come through their door. But that is just not the case.

It is at this point that the police, whether they like it or not, become marriage counselors of a sort. But their goal is not to resolve whatever long-standing problems a couple may have. Rather, they hope to defuse the violent situation well enough so that at least the particular incident is over.

Yet they know similar incidents will probably recur. So does the woman. And that is a source of frustration for both sides. A policeman who has worked in both midwestern and western states summed up the typical patrolman's view of what happens in most domestic disturbance calls:

> They [the women] expect a solution from the police and our solution is, strictly from the perspective of the officer

arriving, to keep the peace. I want to emphasize that—that is all we do, keep the peace. Until such time as someone has been assaulted or one of the parties in the domestic quarrel becomes combative and turns on a police officer, we're not going to arrest anybody. We're here just to simply do no more than a referee at a football game does. We're going to keep the peace, and if we wind up arresting somebody out of that, well, then that is a potential solution to the problem but it is by no means anything that we were sent there to do. Women don't realize that. And when it comes to what advice to tell women, nine times out of ten I'll tell them to go for a civil restraining order and stuff like that, to get a divorce and not stay in the relationship.

Without actually seeing an assault committed the police need a warrant to arrest. Even if a woman has proof of a temporary restraining order in hand, the abusive man is there on the premises, and the police arrive before he leaves, they cannot automatically arrest him. If a man violates a TRO, a woman must return to court and file a motion to find him in contempt of the court. If he is found guilty after a hearing he can be sent to jail for up to six months. But simply having a TRO will not help the woman get the man arrested on the spot. One Fort Worth lawyer did admit that having a TRO could at least pressure the police to take the call for help more seriously: "The only practical effect is that if you have a restraining order and you call the police, I've found they are more apt to come out and at least talk to you ..." [23] But the power of police to arrest in the domestic disturbance situation is much more limited than most people think.

Lack of Training

Most police are poorly trained to deal with domestic disturbances. Much of their professional education deals with the use of firearms and criminal law. Raymond Parnas examined what training most police do receive on the domestic violence problem and found that it mostly consisted of ways they could safeguard themselves in family violence situations. Most policemen could recall from their own training only the statement that such calls can be extremely dangerous and the reminders of the need for caution. Parnas reports:

> The overall emphasis in training seems to be on the danger in handling domestic disturbances. No substantial effort is made to discuss the nature of domestic problems that give rise to such disturbances, the police role in handling these situations, or the available alternatives and their application. Nor is any effort made to explore the particular psychology of these disputes that grows out of the intimate relationship between the disputants. This increases the possibility of danger to the policeman.[24]

The situation across the country is slowly changing. One of the policemen we interviewed had taken a 40-hour class in crisis management, specializing in how to handle domestic disturbance calls. He was even on the advisory board of a family shelter. Others had at least sat through talks and lectures on family violence given by shelter managers and outside consultants.

Dr. Morton Bard, a professor of psychology at the City University of New York and a former New York police officer, has successfully developed a program to teach police domestic intervention skills and make them better informed on how to refer violent couples to social agencies where they can find long-term help. The individual policemen in his pilot units report that they feel more effective when they answer domestic disturbance calls, and safer. And the actual rate of injuries to these police officers decreases noticeably. Moreover, the citizens served appear more satisfied with police handling of calls. Dr. Bard reports:

> There are indirect signs that [the program's] presence has been felt. For one thing, the number of calls for family disturbance intervention has steadily declined over the two-year period, while the number of calls in the comparison precinct has remained constant. One possible explanation is that successful resolution or referral of initial cases has cut

down the chronic or repeat cases. Yet, at the same time, there have been referrals made to the police unit by families who have been served and, hence, some increase might have been expected. The neighborhood grapevine has it that there are some "special family cops" who are O.K. In fact, the men have noted that, when their car rolls into a street (its number is apparently known), people fail to "freeze" as they would when just any police car appears. Also, after initial skepticism, other policemen in the area have grown to respect the work of the unit and to be grateful for its existence.[25]

Does Dr. Bard's training program turn police officers into social workers? He disagrees.

> It is important to note that we did not suggest training police to be social workers or psychologists. Quite the contrary. We suggested that perhaps policemen could be enhanced in doing what they were already doing, while yet retaining their basic identities as working policemen.[26]

More training for handling domestic violence situations, including educating police on the dynamics of abusive relationships so that they can have greater empathy for the battered woman's point of view, is critical. We know it works. The police should be allies of shelter workers in the struggle against domestic violence. After all, no other professionals encounter it so frequently on a day-to-day basis. But unfortunately the groups are more often than not critics of each other. Each side argues that the other does not appreciate the complexities of its situation. Both sides feel frustrated as a result.

POSSIBLE ALTERNATIVES

Most concern about family violence has focused on its victims. Since the turn of the century local governments have seen to it that abused children are cared for. Since the early 1970s privately run shelters, some aided by public funding, have answered battered women's needs as well as their children's. But only recently has much attention been directed to batterers. The huge numbers of women and children applying for admission to the available shelters initially occupied most professionals' attention, but now many are coming to see that the problem will continue to grow, hopelessly unmanageable, unless something is done to cut off violence at its source—the batterers themselves.

Voluntary walk-in programs for abusive men have been established. Some, like EMERGE in Boston, Batterers' Anonymous (which operates similarly to Alcoholics Anonymous) in Redlands, California, and FOCUS in Greensboro, North Carolina, have been successful. Others have not. For example, Friends of the Family, the Denton, Texas, shelter, offered a free counseling service for batterers, but after one year had attracted only one man.

The biggest problem with voluntary programs is that of motivation. The majority of batterers apparently feel they do not have a problem. They believe their violence is justified. Therefore, they are unlikely candidates for counseling programs.

As a result, future plans for reaching batterers and helping them to become nonviolent involve programs that pressure these men into receiving counseling or remaining nonviolent. In the remainder of this chapter we will examine two such efforts. They are examples of how the law could be made effective.

The Family Violence Diversion Network of Austin, Texas

The Austin diversion program began on September 1, 1981. It emerged out of meetings and contacts among a number of agencies that regularly confront different aspects of family violence, such as the Austin Police Department, the Austin Center for Battered Women, the Austin Stress Clinic, and the county attorney's office. Professionals in these groups sensed that their handling of domestic violence was inadequate. In the words of Allen Dietz, a psychologist working with the Austin Police Department:

> We realized that a "hole" existed in the services available for violent families. That hole was that no services existed to help men who batter their spouses or girlfriends. Not only did no services exist, but no leverage existed to encourage the men to seek counseling.

The Family Violence Diversion Network was established to create such leverage. It operates through the municipal court system in the following way:

If a battered woman files a Class C assault charge on her husband or boyfriend, they both will be required to appear at a hearing held in the municipal court. At the hearing the Diversion Network's project coordinator (a trained psychologist) interviews them to see if the man is appropriate for the program (that is, to make sure he is not emotionally unstable or has no long history of violence). If approved, the batterer will then be told that if he pleads guilty or "no contest" to the assault charges he will be allowed to enter the diversion program. If he contests the charges and is found guilty, the municipal court judge can assess the maximum fine ($200) and the man receives a criminal record. But if the man elects to enter the diversion program and successfully completes it, he pays only $50 and does not establish a record.

The program entails group and individual counseling sessions as well as lectures over a six-month period. There are three phases of the program. Phase 1 is a six-week course (1½ hours per week) in stress management, anger control, and relaxation training. The dominant theme is that things and other people do not make the men angry; rather, they choose to become angry and can control their feelings if they wish. Phase 2 is a second six-week course (again 1½ hours per week) presenting the men with information on family problems, sexual stereotypes, and communication skills. Phase 3 consists of 12 weeks of other services tailored to the needs of the individual man and can include alcohol or drug counseling, marriage counseling, and other forms of help. Men are forgiven an occasional absence, but if they deliberately skip sessions or drop out they must go back before the judge and face the maximum punishment.

Funded by the city of Austin and three private foundations with a commitment to stopping family violence (the Levi Strauss Foundation, the Hogg Foundation, and the Meadows Foundation), the program screened 178 men through the Austin municipal court and accepted 92 in its first year. Of those, 62 quit or were dropped from the program because of poor attendance. Approximately 30 men completed it entirely.

Does the program work? It is too early to tell, since there has not been adequate time for follow-ups. Also, the numbers are still very small, partly because only one out of five municipal judges in Austin was willing to cooperate with the program. Is it for every batterer? Definitely not. In the case of the serious abuser the rehabilitation needed is far greater than can be provided by a few short courses on anger control and improving communication skills. The U.S. Commission on Civil Rights considers diversion programs appropriate for moderately abusive men who do not have serious violent or criminal pasts:

> In cases where the pattern of abuse has not yet resulted in serious injury, and where abusers genuinely desire to alter their behavior and have the additional motivation of incarceration for failure to do so, counseling may help them learn how to handle stress without resorting to violence.

But the Commission goes on to note:

> Where defendants are charged with serious or repeat offenses, mandatory counseling is an insufficient sanction.[27]

The program has possibilities. Yet there has been concern, even in persons who helped put the program together, that it will provide many men more chances to beat their wives and then return to the program. They will have accumulated no prior criminal record to alert a judge that they are repeat offenders, as in the case of drivers repeatedly convicted of driving while intoxicated who take specially mandated drivers' education courses to keep their records clean. So far, however, this has not been a problem. There are also accusations that some of the men continue to be violent at home while parroting the anger control "party line" at their weekly meetings. Their wives, it is said, are afraid of more violence to come if they report this or of seeing more serious charges thrown at their husbands.

Without allowing such a program time to work and to correct its weak points before evaluating its effect, we cannot say whether it is a viable alternative to the currently unsuccessful ways we now have of dealing with batterers. But a good many people in Austin are optimistic.

The Interagency Approach

A second, less formal way to pressure batterers into nonviolence and reduce the work loads of everybody dealing with family violence was tried in Dallas during the early 1980s. The frustrations of the courts, the police, and the district attorney's office, and of the many women who called the D.A.'s office for help, were the ones we have been discussing. The police were tired of appearing to be callous and ineffectual, as many women and shelter advocates often consider them to be. The district attorney's office (one female assistant district attorney in particular), which had winning cases as its foremost goal, was frustrated by the enormous number of desperate abused women calling for help and knowing that judges tended to dismiss many abuse cases or hand out lenient sentences. Judges in turn were aware of these criticisms and were also aware of the high numbers of repeat offenders. In short, no one was happy with the state of affairs, and no one had much incentive to apprehend abusers or handle domestic violence cases when they believed other agencies would not back them up.

Coordinated by an assistant district attorney, an informal meeting was held between representatives of the courts, the police, and the district attorney's office. An informal arrangement resulted, which allowed each agency its own rewards, eased the frustrations, and had the potential to reduce repeated violence in some homes. The plan was as follows:

If the police were sent to a home on a domestic disturbance call, either the woman or they would file charges in the district attorney's office if enough evidence existed that an assault had occurred. The assistant district attorney in turn agreed to begin aggressively prosecuting these assault cases, and once charges were filed would not permit a woman to drop them. The police were more willing to handle domestic assault calls once they were assured the cases would not be ignored by the district attorney. If a conviction resulted, the district attorney recommended to the judge that the sentence not be immediately carried out. Instead, the batterer was to be on probation for a period of one year. If at the end of that time he had not had any other complaints or similar assault charges filed against him, the punishment would not be imposed and he would not have a criminal record. If he violated the terms, like the batterers in Austin who dropped out of the diversion program, he earned whatever sentence had been decided and a criminal record. Since most judges in misdemeanor cases, particularly if the case does not involve a jury trial, take the recommendations of prosecutors seriously, the mechanism to end the "repeating" pattern of much domestic violence seemed set in place. The district attorney's office was much more likely to prosecute a domestic assault case knowing a judge was less likely to dismiss it.

Did the plan have any effect? No one knows. It was a logical, workable plan, but shortly after its inception the assistant district attorney responsible went into private practice, by her own admission a victim of "burn out" over the issue of family violence. She had been the only lawyer in the D.A.'s office to operate according to the plan. Without her or someone else determined to make it work, the other two agencies were back to where they started, which unfortunately is where they are today.

This second plan, like the diversion program, illustrates an important point about ways to combat the family problem through the legal system. Despite the fact that there are many official agencies that could work together as allies in the struggle, often they do not cooperate. Either they cannot understand how to, or they are victims of bureaucratic "turfism," jealous of keeping a monopoly on whatever goes on in their jurisdiction. They thus take a narrow view of how best to get their own rewards, disregarding the larger picture. In an era when taxpayers and legislators cast a critical eye on any agency whose services overlap with any other, this is understandable.

So, as in any other social movement, innovation has to come from dynamic individuals who will push for it, and who will make a new way of doing things their own private crusade. After a point the mechanisms they set up can function smoothly without them, like small businesses that grow into industries. But in the beginning those individuals are extremely important. If they leave the formal or informal program too soon, it can founder. We have seen this in other social service programs, and it will be just as true in the movement to mobilize the law to help victims of family violence.

8

A LOOK AHEAD

Henry Ford, the great industrialist and inventor of the American automobile, once remarked that "History is bunk." What he meant, of course, is that there are no lessons in history to help us predict the future, much less understand the present. This man who knew so much about the production of combustion engines was amazingly pessimistic (and naive) about humanity's ability to profit from its own experience.

This position is absurd. A moment's thought will show that we use our personal experience every day in making decisions and choosing courses of action. We make investments, size up situations, raise our children, and perform our jobs on the basis of experience. The implication of this fact for us is that families can learn ways to settle their conflicts without resorting to physical force; the key is providing men and women with a means of developing a personal history of nonphysical techniques. In the beginning it has to be seen as a skills problem, or in the end it will become a criminal problem.

But in this concluding chapter we do not intend to examine the various theories and therapies current among social workers and psychologists of the anger management school of thought. Enough has been written elsewhere about positive alternatives to violence as a way of settling family disputes. Instead, we want to review what our research has revealed and discuss what it means for the future study of family violence. We would also like to suggest some very basic, immediate actions that any concerned citizen can take that will help improve the current situation. Finally, we will evaluate what serious violence between men and their families means for our society as a whole.

We *can* learn from history, and we can use it to shape the future.

THE TIP OF THE ICEBERG

The violence we have documented with statistical trends and personal anecdotes represents virtually only the tip of the family violence iceberg. From the number of calls to the shelters and their long waiting lists we know there are many thousands of seriously abused women in the Dallas–Fort Worth Metroplex alone. The nationwide situation is staggering to imagine. No shelter coordinator, director, or staff person that we know or that we have read of anywhere in the United States believes otherwise.

We approached this problem with as comprehensive a set of information as we could possibly gather. We obtained details about women, their children, and their abusive men. We studied how family shelters operate, their problems, and their goals. We examined women from different backgrounds, rural and urban, lower- and middle-class, of many races, ages, and income levels. We asked questions of different professionals who confront the family violence problem about how they perceive it. These persons included lawyers, judges, policemen, social workers, and counselors. We did not limit ourselves only to women who enter shelters to find safety. We also interviewed battered women who had not gone through shelters in order to see how similar the conditions of violence were in their homes. What we learned reinforces many of the impressions that more clinically oriented social workers and psychologists working with the problem have formed. Our study also challenges some of the conventional wisdom about family violence.

We found that serious family violence indeed cuts across all social classes and virtually every other division one can think of in American society. In fact, there are signs that some types of violence, including sexual abuse, are more severe and frequent in middle-class families than in low-income homes. Not all women who experience violence eventually make it to a public shelter, but the ones who do fit no stereotype of "welfare mothers," neither are they women who want anything other than a traditional homemaking career. The majority of these women are young mothers, and their predicament cannot be explained away by blaming their failure to get along with their men on feminist ideas.

A further myth that we hope we have laid to rest is that these women have not had to confront real violence. Much of the violence is more severe, even grotesque, than most people can easily imagine. Christine M. deLange, executive coordinator of Dallas's Family Place, commented to us once that when she gave workshop presentations on family violence to other social workers and counselors less familiar with the problem, they were initially incredulous at the extreme levels of abuse that women and children who come to shelters regularly suffer. Certainly the grisly parade of stories that we have presented does not begin to exhaust the nightmarish tales that shelter workers and residents can tell.

An important finding in our study is the failure of the generational transfer hypothesis to help explain either why these women became involved with violent men or why they endured their wrath for considerable periods of time. According to the women's own memories of their parents and childhoods (which, though we know them to be imperfect, are the best and only information we currently have), they do not appear to have been taught that a woman's role in marriage is to be hit. Rather, their marriages to violent men are probably simply a matter of bad luck (as psychologist Lenore Walker has suggested), because there are so many violent men out there to begin with. The women did not leave their homes immediately after violence began not because they were masochists but often because they wanted to try to make the marriage work or they saw no alternatives. When they discovered at least one viable alternative (a shelter), they did leave, often quickly.

The most recent similar study to ours, that of sociologist Mildred Pagelow, also primarily used shelter residents for information. She also found that the generational transfer hypothesis is more useful for understanding men's battering than women's victimization.[1] This suggests that recent research is beginning to converge and adds to our confidence that the cases we examined were not unique. In other words, blaming the victim to explain why women are battered does not work any better than it would to explain child abuse. When violent families are not randomly picked but come to our attention selectively, our knowledge of the problem depends heavily on repeated similar studies. In family violence research we are now accumulating this kind of reliable scientific information.

Woman-battering has often been thought of as a separate problem from child abuse, but as we have seen the two are closely related. Usually, if there are children living in a home where a man is beating a woman, they too will become victims. In addition to the high rate of physical abuse of children, emotional abuse is also rampant. In Chapter five we mentioned an incident that occurred in one south Texas shelter: an angry husband broke in and roamed the building, berserk with rage, looking for his spouse. One staff member who witnessed it made the telling observation that amid the smashing of windows and terrified screams of women the children became deathly still, suddenly aware again of the familiar tension and expectation of violence. Particularly among boys, there is a good chance that exposure to, and experience with, such violence will have a long-lasting effect.

Before this study not much had been known about the batterer aside from clinical speculation about his personality. We now have a much better picture of the violent men who have literally driven women out of their homes and into shelters. They may not be typical of all batterers, but these men are the men responsible for filling publicly supported shelters and clogging their waiting lists. Such a batterer is often a domineering man who is violent to others besides the woman. He frequently drinks or takes drugs, at least when he is violent, and very probably has been in trouble with the law. His behavior after battering episodes is sometimes affectionate or repentant, but half the time he feels justified in being violent. And if he feels justified he tends to batter the woman more severely.

A woman has two basic options when she is beaten: to leave or to stay. In either case she is then confronted with other choices. Many of these choices are often not very good ones from her standpoint, and at best can only produce short-term relief. The police, the courts, the district attorney, even the clergy offer little in the way of meaningful solutions. Most women cannot simply run, move out, or murder the violent man. The shelter choice, on the other hand, can provide both temporary help and long-run solutions, for we have seen that the knowledge that women are willing to leave and have a place to go forces some men to reconsider their violence.

Moreover, there are ways that courts and other agencies can directly attack the roots of violence in the home. We described a few innovative programs that now exist or have existed. Judges can pressure known batterers to go through treatment programs. District attorneys' offices can cooperate with judges and police to use real prosecution as a means to break the cycle of violence in a home, discouraging battering by threat of criminal prosecution or punishing batterers who are unwilling to change. Once such officials accept the family violence problem as more than a sensational set of isolated incidents or merely a nuisance, they may be more willing to consider these practical alternatives.

WHAT CAN BE DONE?

Our analysis paints a grim picture, but family violence is not like the weather. Such violent acts are not of God but of men. Therefore something can be done. Recommendations for what can be done have become the obligatory last chapters of virtually all books on domestic violence. Our suggestions are pragmatic and modest. We do not call for crusades to change the way all men regard women, or to reform our entire legal system, or to pass Constitutional amendments, or to ban violent themes in media and literature, or to deglorify contact sports. Such sweeping changes are largely unrealistic. We offer the following recommendations, which many average citizens can act on immediately.

First, legislators do pay attention to those constituents who contact them, particularly if those constituents do not seem to be part of the lunatic fringe and if enough persons convey similar messages. On the long list of legislators' priorities, family violence frequently gets pushed toward the bottom. Legislators, like almost everyone else, are usually unaware of the true extent of family violence. But they can be informed and reminded. Funding for various programs to help women, children, and batterers will only assume a higher priority or urgency when legislators perceive a serious bloc of voters concerned with it. Write or call them. The same can be said about every judge and state attorney general who runs for office. Make family violence part of his or her electoral agenda.

Second, the public at large also needs to be educated about family violence, particularly its scope and frequency and its dynamics (how and why it seems to happen). It is true that social scientists have not answered all our questions about these issues, but we are no longer operating in the dark. This sort of education should be provided by the schools and the churches. However, the churches (as we noted in Chapter five) have a long way to go in recognizing and dealing with family violence. Clergy need to attend workshops, and seminaries need to include the subject in pastoral counseling courses. Likewise, public schools have thus far been of little help. Most junior and senior high schools offer courses in home economics or health, and even progressive courses that try to expose teenagers to the realities of adult living (such as drawing up family budgets, paying taxes, and dividing up homemaking responsibilities). But it would be a rare course indeed that discussed child abuse and woman-battering or included anger management techniques among its topics. The only course possibly relevant to domestic violence is self-defense, and it is taught as physical education, not home economics. Public education is slightly better at the university level where some instructors in the social sciences make use of guest lectures, films, and available books to alert students to the problem of family violence. But this reaches only one limited part of the general population.

Third, family shelters in every community are always short of funds and operate on shoestring budgets. For example, as we saw in Chapter six, the Texas Department of Human Resources provides an average shelter with only one fourth of its budget. The rest must be made up from local United Way agencies, grants from foundations and local businesses, and individual contributions. But anyone can help support a shelter in a number of ways. For instance:

- Urge state legislators to support shelter allotments in annual or biennial budgets. Nowhere are allotted funds nearly adequate, so the larger the recommendations the better.
- Target donations to the United Way to be used for local shelters. This will help ensure that they receive their maximum United Way allotment.
- Give privately to the shelters (such gifts are tax-deductible). Not only money but clothes, books, furniture, and toys are needed.
- Volunteer to spend an hour or two per week as a telephone counselor or doing odd jobs; offer to drive shelter residents to job interviews or other appointments.

There are many more ways to help. Civic organizations can contribute money and churches can be mobilized for volunteer work as happened in both Denton and Dallas. All such groups can be encouraged to sponsor speakers from local shelters to create better awareness of family violence *in that community,* and honoraria for the speakers can be donated directly to the shelters. As we were writing the above suggestions we read about how a local Girl Scout troop established a program to escort the children of battered women in one shelter to YWCAs and parks and to plan a Christmas party for shelter children. There are many organizations such as the Girl Scouts in almost every American community, and they all have the goal of community service. Make sure that they know the family shelter is one of the agencies that needs volunteer help.

These suggestions are fairly prosaic. They entail no sweeping, grand overhauls of our legal system nor radical changes in our society. By themselves they will do nothing directly to end family violence. We admit that, at least at first glance, they seem to be ways of coping with the problem rather than solving it. There are, of course, other important actions that need to be taken by professionals in the courts, in district attorneys' offices, in legislative staff offices, and in hospitals and schools that can attack the sources of family violence more directly. Chapter seven indicated some of these. But these require time, expertise, or a level of commitment that the average person simply does not have. But if many people were to follow through on just one or two of our suggestions at the local level, each shelter's burden would be significantly lighter. And since we know that the fact of a woman's leaving violence in her home can noticeably decrease or end future violence, enlarging any shelter's capabilities does do more than simply cope with the problem. It directly attacks the cause as well.

There are a number of false and vicious myths about what shelters do, such as that they tear apart families and encourage divorce or that they give haven to lazy homemakers, but like all myths these can be shown to be false. The tragedy is that persons in power—mayors, city council members, and legislators, to name a few—believe them. The community (not merely the shelter) is the loser. For family violence is a public health problem as assuredly as is the contamination of the water supply.

THE CULT OF VIOLENCE AND THE FAMILY

But what is the larger meaning of the horrible anecdotes and violent patterns we have discovered? If family violence, as we have described it, is so prevalent, what can we expect of the future? What can sociologists, who deal with groups, say about a problem rooted so deeply in individuals?

Many people have taken pretty much for granted since the dawn of the industrial age that with the development of scientific technology our society will become more civilized. That is, humaneness and reason will supposedly continue to replace violence just as contracts have replaced handshakes and lawsuits have replaced gunfights and duels. In Shakespeare's day one popular form of entertainment was bear-baiting: a bear was thrown into a deep pit and slowly stabbed to death with poles as an amused crowd looked on and cheered. That sort of brutality may have been fine in Elizabethan England, one can say, but in our modern era such acts are regarded as cruel. Except in some rural pockets of the United States where they still thrive illegally, dog-fighting, cock-fighting, and other abuse of animals for "sport" have been successfully outlawed.

Thus to a certain extent it is true that our society has discouraged many forms of violence that used to be more acceptable and commonplace. But we also know that more sophisticated technology has by no means made severe violence extinct. On the international level it has left us the nightmarish legacy of possible nuclear war which, despite the facile assurances of our policy makers, promises complete annihilation of our civilization. That destructive potential, added to the multinational pressures of revolutions, expansionist invasions, and religious fanaticism, has ensured that violence among nations cannot possibly wither away in the foreseeable future.

Many forms of aggression have gone underground and resurfaced in the home, among intimates. For many women and children the chances of being raped, beaten, or even murdered are greater in their bedrooms than out on impersonal city streets in our largest urban centers. We know the long history of family violence. It has been a part of western civilization from the very beginning. There can be no illusion that it is on the decline. But is it true that we are simply more aware of such violence in the home and more sensitive to it? Or is it possible that this type of violence, always present to some extent, is on the increase?

There is no definite way to tell. However, we think there is good reason to believe that a cult of violence is spreading throughout our society and affecting every sector. By "cult" we do not mean that it is an organized movement or conspiracy. Rather, it is a cultural pattern, a trend. The glorification of violence in motion pictures, television, and books, and the electronic media's technical sophistication that shows us violence realistically but makes it exciting, contribute to this cult. But this is not the cause. The cult is an acceptance of violence, learning to expect it, to tolerate it, and to commit it, however much one dreads it. This cult is stimulated by a violent environment that affects each generation of men and women, making them more yet desensitized to the problem. Jean Renvoize came to a similar conclusion in her book *Web of Violence* when she wrote of the steady atmosphere of violence to which we all have become so accustomed:

> Violence has entered our lives to a degree that would have been unthinkable even a decade ago. Terrorist attacks, political kidnappings, bombs indiscriminately exploded among innocent civilians; all these horrors which once only happened to other people now are part of our own experience.

> There are periodic scares about mugging in the streets, and there is no doubt that adolescent crime has risen to a frightening extent. It could be that the growing acceptance of information about violence in the home (previously a subject about which no one wanted to know) is partly an attempt to shrink this world-wide expression of violence down to more familiar proportions.[2]

There are many ominous signs that a cult of violence is spreading: our declining sense of horror when yet another important world figure, even a president or a pope, is attacked or assassinated; our smooth adaptation to being searched and x-rayed like potential criminals every time we travel by airplane because of the dangers of terrorism; the willingness of many perfectly decent, sane individuals to talk calmly about the tens of millions of Americans who might survive a nuclear war while the majority of us are incinerated and the ecology of the planet is destroyed; our response to the proliferation of weapons in the United States by simply going out to gun shops and arming ourselves as well; the rise in reported child- and woman-battering; even the shocking increase in physical abuse of the elderly by their own grown children.

There are other signs. One of them is an increase in seemingly irrational violence such as shown in our study. Some women who appear at shelters have not merely been beaten. They have been humiliated in horrible ways, such as having had men urinate on them. One woman's husband smeared dog feces in her hair and face. Outside the shelters violence increasingly takes strange forms that raise an eyebrow, but only temporarily. As we wrote this book one incident in Dallas that is admittedly bizarre (although in one year in any reasonably large American city you could easily collect a number of such ghastly stories) came to light. Police found a terrified woman who had been kidnapped and held captive for a week in a second-story Dallas apartment. She had escaped by tying bedspreads together and breaking a bathroom window, lowering herself to the ground. She led police back and they found a second woman (from Michigan) who had been held captive for *nine months*. The *Fort Worth Star-Telegram* reported:

The apartment was decorated with pornographic photographs and Dallas Cowboys memorabilia, and it was littered with trash and homemade sex devices, police said. Boards had been nailed across the three windows in the apartment, and the hallway was decorated with women's underwear. Investigators also discovered logging chains, an 18-inch piece of pipe and bloody sticks. Mingled in with the pornography were pictures of Elvis Presley and Jesus Christ, police said.

"It's amazing. It's pitiful," police Sgt. E. L. Whitfield said. "In my nine years of experience, when I walked in, all I could say was, 'Oh, my God.' It was such a shock." Whitfield called the apartment a "semi-torture chamber" from which it "was almost impossible to escape."

The Michigan woman was "almost to the point of being crazy, he had her so intimidated," Whitfield said. The women, covered with cuts and bruises, told police they had been chained by their necks, beaten with sticks and pipes, and raped and sexually abused. Police said the man had cropped the women's hair almost to the scalp. "He cut their hair so they would be less attractive and would not try to escape . . ." The women told police that the man padlocked the only door to the apartment when he left.

A resident of the small, dilapidated apartment complex said she knew the women were being held captive, but she and others failed to heed their screams. "You could hear her hollering and him beating them," said Sona Minnieweather, whose apartment faces the suspect's across a vacant lot. "You could hear them women all through the day." Ms. Minnieweather said she talked to one of the women through a window on Thursday evening. "She said they hadn't ate nothing in a week and that she was chained down. She said she'd give us $50 to call the police, but I thought she was drunk . . ."

Bob Shaw, a police spokesman, said that "residents of this part of town just don't get involved in other peoples' business—they are just afraid or something." [3]

From the standpoint of understanding the cult of violence in our society, the kidnapper's sado-sexual actions are not as revealing as the neighbors' reaction to the women's abuse. The woman quoted above *knew* a great deal of violence was being committed. As in the publicized case of Kitty Genovese in New York City some years ago, when that young woman was stabbed to death in the street below while apartment dwellers watched from their windows and did nothing, this Dallas woman did not even take the trouble to call the police, much less intervene herself.

Any simple explanation of this cult of violence is impossible. Some factors that might seem to be causes, such as the media's emphasis on the thrill and glamour of spectacular destruction (the obligatory multi-car chase-and-crash sequences in police shows, for instance), are probably no more than reflections of popular taste and the tolerance of violence. Other factors, like economic pressure during recessions, only worsen existing violence but again do not cause it. As in asking why men batter, here too there are both psychological and sociological aspects that have to be considered together if the epidemic's causes and effects are going to be successfully monitored and contained. Understanding the limits of the generational transfer hypothesis to explain current violence, for example, can help therapists approach each battered woman or child with more realistic assumptions. Sociology's contribution may well be to single out those factors in the social context that contribute to family violence, factors that we may never be able to say conclusively cause violence but which we know accompany it and which can be taken into account in trying to reduce it.

In this book we have discussed many of these factors, such as the economic marginality of many young batterers and their underemployed or unemployed wives, the poor economy, and the frequent lack of human relations skills for settling differences peacefully. Yet we also know that many of these same factors are not relevant to middle- and upper-class homes where violence also occurs. The social context is different there and other factors need to be considered. It is an axiom in sociology that nothing is distributed equally: not wealth, not poverty, not misery. Nor are the same causes of violence found in every violent family.

We all live in a social context that breeds frustration, and as psychologists have known for decades, one probable (though not inevitable) consequence of frustration is aggression, or violence. This aggression seems to be directed at a wide range of targets in many situations in our society, and indications are that it is increasing. The fast-paced urban lifestyle and "boom-town" mentality of citizens in Dallas, Texas, for example, is undoubtedly one factor producing in that city a suicide rate between 23 and 50 percent higher than the national average, according to different estimates. Dallas's divorce rate is one of the highest in the nation. Its congested freeways and access roads are often the scenes of violence between motorists who become involved in minor accidents or are simply discourteous to one another. Simply passing another car in a slow lane, or cutting off a car too abruptly when changing lanes, can result in shootings, stabbings, windshields smashed with tire irons, and fistfights. The same is true in other large cities. One Houston homicide detective reported: "We've had as many as two and three killings in a month's time that arose from nothing more than [the honk of a horn] . . . It started seven or eight years ago in California. They called it freeway assaults."

The city of Houston's newly formed Major Assaults Unit chief gave the example of one middle-aged man who was dragged from his car and kicked repeatedly simply because he had signaled another driver to dim the high beams on his headlights. He concluded, "It's an attitude problem if you're getting so mad that you shoot a finger at somebody who honks his horn when you're too slow to reacting to a light . . ." [4]

The importance of the social context where violence occurs, seen in the few examples above and in the argument presented in Chapter three that the American family and its values actually make the possibility of child abuse likely, suggests that the very way our technologically advanced society has emerged actually produces frustrations that become translated into violence. An end to the pressures and frustrations caused by dealing with vast, faceless bureaucracies where the buck never stops anywhere, living in overpopulated communities, and dealing with many underpaid public servants is nowhere in sight.

Even when violence does not begin in the home it can still affect family members, reinforcing the use of aggression to deal with frustrations. For example, as we finished our research a controversy erupted in Fort Worth, Texas, public schools over the practice of paddling children. While school systems in various cities such as Washington, D.C., New York, Baltimore, and Chicago have regulations against corporal punishment and some states such as Massachusetts and New Jersey have forbidden it, it is still common in the southwest. A newspaper article reported the following from parents who complained when their eleven-year-old son was struck three times on the buttocks with a wooden paddle:

> "I am not against punishing a child for what he did, but I am against leaving marks," the mother said. "I would be against my husband leaving marks."
> "They'd throw me underneath the jailhouse if I did my own child the way they did," the father said. "I'm for whipping kids to make them mind, but I don't leave bruises on them."

While school officials denied the boy had been bruised, a Fort Worth Civil Liberties Union spokesperson noted that much physical discipline goes undocumented. He added, "We hear about some rather capricious use of corporal punishment . . . We had one report from West Texas where a fourth-grade girl was paddled for doing her spelling homework incorrectly." [5]

From the teachers' and administrators' positions there are too many behavior problems, too few teachers, and increasing strains between the teaching profession and the local community, so paddling becomes a quick, easy way of temporarily removing the class disturbance. But using aggression in this way is not effective and only adds to the problem in the long run. It is no coincidence that so many men and women are abandoning the teaching profession as the pressures for them either to use or not use aggression against students mount, forcing them into a "damned-if-you-do-damned-if-you-don't" dilemma.

Some people learn to deal with these strains philosophically or they construct self-help strategies, such as jogging or karate. Or they become so emotionally detached from their work and others that they seem almost like automatons. Others take their frustrations home where other problems will naturally arise in due course. There are many elements spreading the cult of violence into the family at an increasing rate, including a deteriorating economy that pressures women to become supplementary (if not equal) wage earners, an unwillingness of many women automatically to defer to male authority, and the short-run effectiveness of violence in stifling arguments. It is important to remember that these strains inflame, but do not cause, violence in the family. The economic independence of working women, the women's liberation movement, or the Equal Rights Amendment movement may be blamed for women increasingly becoming unwilling to endure domestic violence, but the real cause of such violence is in the belief that men have the right to use violence against other members of their family. It may be a belief born out of an assumption of male superiority or spawned by the fact that men have greater physical bulk than women or inspired by sadism. However, the cult of violence only feeds this belief. Outside forces, apart from the family, do not cause it.

There is no reason to think the growth of violence is slowing. The world is witnessing a mammoth wave of changes that human beings have no previous experience with. And our ability to adapt as a species is not infinite; the spectre of nuclear war shows us that clearly. Family violence is one symptom of humans' unsuccessful struggle with the increasing pressures to adapt to their technologically complex society. Ironically, coping with such pressures by rechanneling them through violence in the home may ultimately squelch our chances for survival at all, for no society of any consequence can survive if its family institution crumbles from within.

Appendices

Notes

Select Bibliography
on Family Violence

Index

Appendix A

Tables for This Study

CHAPTER 2. WOMEN: THE MOST VISIBLE VICTIMS

TABLE 2-1: FORMS OF BATTERING AMONG SHELTER RESIDENTS 1980–82 *

Forms of Battering	N	%
Slaps	447	83
Kicks	336	62
Punches	406	75
Burns	61	11
Sexual abuse	136	25
Threats to use weapon	281	52
Use of weapon	116	21
Other	137	25
Battered while pregnant	229	42
Choking	51	9

* Residents frequently experience multiple forms of violence.
Total = 542.

TABLE 2-2: TYPE OF INJURIES AMONG SHELTER RESIDENTS 1980–82 *

Type of Injury	N	%
Broken glasses	35	7
Bruises	450	83
Cuts	235	43
Broken bones	118	22
Burns	49	9
Other	76	14
Complications with pregnancy	42	8

* Residents may experience multiple injuries.
Total = 542.

TABLE 2-3: SUMMARY OF CHARACTERISTICS OF SHELTER RESIDENTS *

Marital Status	N	%
Married	385	72
Separated	49	9
Divorced	6	1
Not married/living together	72	13
Not married/not living together	14	3
Other	12	2
TOTAL	538	100

Number of Marriages	N	%
0	56	10
1	318	59
2	134	25
3	25	5
4	8	2
5	1	.2
TOTAL	542	100

TABLE 2-3: (CONTINUED)

Education of Residents	N	%
Less than high school	212	39
High school/some college	300	56
College and above	25	5
TOTAL	537	100

Ethnicity	N	%
White-Anglo	343	64
Black	117	22
Hispanic	56	10
Native American	10	2
Oriental	3	1
Other	9	2
TOTAL	538	100

Income if Employed Outside Home	N	%
$0– $4,999	99	40
$5,000– $7,499	51	21
$7,500– $9,999	33	13
$10,000–$14,999	34	14
$15,000–$19,999	1	.4
$20,000–$24,999	1	.4
$25,000–$29,999	1	.4
$30,000+	26	11
TOTAL	246	100

Occupation	N	%
Unemployed/homemaker	294	56
Clerical/sales/skilled labor	132	25
Unskilled labor	55	11
Military/professional/farm	42	8
TOTAL	523	100

TABLE 2-3: (CONTINUED)

Have Money on Hand	N	%
Yes	345	64
No	195	36
TOTAL	540	100

Amount of Money on Hand	N	%
$0– $20	236	68
$21– $50	53	15
$51–$100	25	7
$100+	31	9
TOTAL	345	100

Alcohol-Related Problems	N	%
Yes	23	4
No	499	96
TOTAL	522	100

Drug-Related Problems	N	%
Yes	15	3
No	511	97
TOTAL	526	100

* As is common with most questionnaires, for a variety of reasons not every question was always answered. Thus, the percentages reported refer only to those women who responded to that particular item.

TABLE 2-4: VIOLENCE IN SHELTER RESIDENTS' CHILDHOOD FAMILIES

Existence of Spouse Abuse Between Parents	N	%
Yes	172	34
No	332	66

Resident Abused as a Child	N	%
Yes	134	26
No	387	74

Resident Neglected as a Child	N	%
Yes	90	21
No	345	79

Resident's Mother Had Alcohol Problem	N	%
Yes	59	12
No	451	88

Resident's Father Had Alcohol Problem	N	%
Yes	145	29
No	362	71

TABLE 2-5: FREQUENCY AND DURATION OF ABUSE TO SHELTER RESIDENTS

Frequency of Battering	N	%
First time	25	4
Less than twice a year	26	5
Less than once a month	88	17
1–3 times a month	178	35
More than once a week	134	26
Daily	62	12
TOTAL	513	100

Tolerated abuse for	N	%
Less than 6 months	58	13
6 months–11 months	57	13
1 year–2 years	127	28
3 years–5 years	91	20
5 years and over	121	26
TOTAL	454	100

TABLE 2-6: ISSUES ASSOCIATED WITH BATTERING AMONG SHELTER RESIDENTS 1980–82 *

Issue	N	%
Alcohol/drugs	381	70
Sex demands	143	26
Job pressure (financial)	316	58
Jealousy	360	66
Pregnancy	75	14
Family	86	16
Other	10	2

* Violent episode may be result of more than one issue.
Total = 542.

TABLE 2-7: FACTORS CAUSING SHELTER RESIDENTS TO STAY 1980–82 *

Reasons for Staying	N	%
Loved him	83	15
Because of children	111	21
Economic dependency	165	30
Coerced into staying	78	14
Thought she could save marriage	144	27
Other	86	16

* Several battered women gave two reasons for staying.
Total = 542.

CHAPTER 3. CHILDREN: THE MOST HELPLESS VICTIMS

TABLE 3-1: AGE AND FREQUENCY OF CHILDREN IN VIOLENT HOMES

Age	N	%
1 year old or less	179	19
2–3	211	23
4–5	116	13
6–7	100	11
8–9	110	12
10–11	96	10
12+	108	12
TOTAL	920	100

Mean = 5.75.
Median = 5.2.

TABLE 3-2: CHILDREN AWARE OF, OR WITNESS,
THE PHYSICAL ABUSE OF THEIR MOTHER

Yes		No		TOTAL	
N	%	N	%	N	%
379	89	45	11	424	100

TABLE 3-3: TYPE OF ABUSE EXPERIENCED
BY CHILDREN *

Form of Abuse	N	%
Verbal abuse	217	51
Slaps	151	36
Kicks	34	8
Punches	47	11
Burns	3	1
Sexual abuse	12	3
Other	55	13

* Child could experience multiple forms of abuse.

TABLE 3-4: TYPE OF INJURIES EXPERIENCED
BY CHILDREN

Type of Injury	N	%
Bruises	121	64
Cuts	35	18
Broken bones	9	5
Burns	3	2
Other	22	11
TOTAL	190	100

TABLE 3-5: HOW LONG CHILD ABUSE
HAS BEEN OCCURRING

Length of Time	N	%
Less than 1 year	52	32
1–2 years	49	30
3–4 years	25	15
5–6 years	15	9
7 years and over	22	14
TOTAL	163	100

TABLE 3-6: HOW OFTEN DOES
CHILD ABUSE OCCUR

Frequency	N	%
First time	26	15
Less than twice a year	22	13
Less than once a month	24	14
1–3 times a month	34	20
1 or more times a week	40	23
Daily	25	15
TOTAL	171	100

CHAPTER 4. MEN: THE PERPETRATORS OF VIOLENCE

TABLE 4-1: CHARACTERISTICS OF THE BATTERERS

Education	N	%
Less than high school	213	43
High school/some college	257	52
College degree and above	22	5
TOTAL	492	100

Occupation	N	%
Unemployed/homemaker	74	15
Clerical/sales/skilled labor	258	51
Unskilled labor	119	24
Military/professional/farmer	53	11
TOTAL	504	100

Income*	N	%
Less than $4,999	49	15
$5,000– $7,499	42	13
$7,500– $9,999	48	15
$10,000–$14,999	87	26
$15,000–$19,999	37	11
$20,000–$24,999	24	7
$25,000–$29,999	7	2
$30,000–$40,000	7	2
$40,000+	31	9
TOTAL	332	100

Ethnicity	N	%
White-Anglo	309	58
Black	136	25
Hispanic	62	12
Other	26	5
TOTAL	533	100

* 210 residents did not know or refused to answer question on income.

TABLE 4-2: OTHER FORMS OF VIOLENT BEHAVIOR OF THE BATTERER

Violent Toward	N	%
Animals	60	13
Children	97	20
Objects	115	24
Children and objects	48	10
Animals and objects	58	12
Other	39	8
Not violent	64	13
TOTAL	481	100

TABLE 4-3: ARREST OR CONVICTION OF BATTERER

Arrest Record	N	%
Assault against client	33	7
Violence against others	115	26
Assault against client and others	31	7
Other criminal activity	151	34
Driving while intoxicated	34	8
Never arrested/convicted	86	19.1
TOTAL	450	100

TABLE 4-4: FREQUENCY DISTRIBUTION OF VIOLENCE OR ABUSE IN BATTERER'S FAMILY OF ORIENTATION

Batterer's Experiences	Response	Frequency	%
Spouse abuse between	Yes	244	57
batterer's parents	No	181	42
Batterer abused as	Yes	160	38
a child	No	258	61
Batterer neglected	Yes	151	40
as a child	No	223	59
Batterer's siblings	Yes	94	31
abused as children	No	206	69
Mother with alcohol-	Yes	101	22
related problems	No	356	77
Father with alcohol-	Yes	226	49
related problems	No	231	50

TABLE 4-5: FEELINGS OF BATTERER AFTER EPISODE * (AMONG SHELTER RESIDENTS 1980–82)

Feelings of Batterer	N	%
Beatings justified	267	49
Leaves home	139	25
Apologizes	340	63
Acts affectionately	240	44
Does favor	148	27
Other	84	16
None of the above	9	2

* Batterers express multiple emotions following a violent episode.
Total = 542.

CHAPTER 5. AFTER THE BATTERING: A WOMAN'S OPTIONS

TABLE 5-1: WERE POLICE CALLED? (HOTLINE TELEPHONE CALLS, 1980–82)

	N	%
Yes	829	44.7
No	1027	55.3

Total = 1856.

TABLE 5-2: DID THE POLICE RESPOND? (HOTLINE TELEPHONE CALLS, 1980–82)

	N	%
Yes	537	69.0
No	241	31.0

Total = 778.

TABLE 5-3: TYPE OF ABUSE AMONG HELP-CENTER CLIENTS *

Form of Abuse	N	%
Verbal	67	100
Slaps	54	80
Kicks	37	55
Punches	46	69
Burns	6	9
Sex abuse	20	30
Choking	36	54
Threats with weapon	35	52
Battered while pregnant	25	37
Destroyed property	39	58
Other	24	36

* Clients experienced multiple forms of battering.

TABLE 5-4: TYPES OF INJURIES AMONG HELP-CENTER CLIENTS *

Type of Injury	N	%
Bruises	57	85
Cuts	31	46
Broken bones	14	21
Burns	4	6
Black eye	8	12

* Clients experienced multiple injuries.

TABLE 5-5: HELP-CENTER CLIENTS' REASONS FOR STAYING IN RELATIONSHIP

Reasons	N	%
Love him	13	20
Because of children	4	6
Promise to change	1	2
Economic reasons	2	3
Afraid to leave	4	6
Family pressure	5	8
Other	37	55
TOTAL	66	100

TABLE 5-6: REASONS FOR COMING TO HELP CENTER *

Reasons	N	%
Counseling	30	56
Information and referral	16	30
Moral support	32	59
Education	1	2
Others	2	4

* Several women gave more than one reason.
Total = 54.

Appendix B

The CSR Severity Index

THE CSR (CENTER FOR SOCIAL RESEARCH) SEVERITY INDEX

We considered severity of physical abuse to be an important factor in analyzing the problems of battered women. We therefore developed the CSR Severity Index. It consists of two types of measures: (1) the forms of battering experienced by a woman; and (2) the types of injuries inflicted on her. We assigned weighted values that indicate the seriousness of battering and injuries, with higher values for actions and injuries that would put the woman's life in actual jeopardy. The listing of battering forms, injuries, and point values is as follows:

Battering Forms

Verbal abuse/threats	1
Slaps	2
Kicks	3
Punches	4
Burns	5
Sexual abuse	6
Battered while pregnant	7
Choking	8
Other*	9
Threats to use weapon	10
Use of weapon	11

* Usually involved fairly serious forms of battering and injury.

Types of Injuries (Physical)

None	0
Broken glasses	1
Bruises	2
Cuts	3
Burns	4
Broken bones	5
Complications with pregnancy	6
Other	7

The points for all forms of battering and types of injuries inflicted in each case are added together to create a Severity Index Score. Scores could range from 1 to 94.

For purposes of analysis, we also divided the cases into high severity and low severity groups. Individual cases with severity scores greater than 15 were placed in the high-severity group, the others in the low-severity group. We used 15 rather than the mean score of 29 or the median score of 27, because in order to compile a severity score of greater than 15 the batterer would have to engage in violence that would be potentially life-threatening to the woman. Verbal abuse, it is true, could do more harm in the long run than many forms of physical battering, but our criteria, like those of shelters, were those of the woman's physical safety.

Notes

1: BEYOND THE BURNING BED

1. Faith McNulty, *The Burning Bed* (New York: Harcourt Brace Jovanovich, 1980).
2. Readers are referred to the selected bibliography at the end of this book.
3. Richard J. Gelles, *The Violent Home: A Study of Physical Aggression Between Husbands and Wives* (Beverly Hills, Ca.: SAGE Publications, 1974).
4. Murray A. Straus, Richard J. Gelles, and Suzanne K. Steinmetz, *Behind Closed Doors: Violence in the American Family* (Garden City, N.Y.: Anchor/Doubleday, 1980), 32.
5. Straus, Gelles, and Steinmetz, *Behind Closed Doors: Violence in the American Family*.
6. Suzanne K. Steinmetz, "The Battered Husband Syndrome," *Victimology: An International Journal* 2, nos. 3–4 (1977–78): 499–509; and "Wife-Beating, Husband-Beating—A Comparison of the Use of Physical Violence Between Spouses to Resolve Marital Fights," in *Battered Women*, ed. Maria Roy (New York: Van Nostrand Reinhold, 1977), 63–72.
7. Naomi F. Chase, *A Child Is Being Beaten* (New York: McGraw-Hill, 1975), 1.
8. William Ryan, *Blaming the Victim*, rev. ed. (New York: Vintage Books, 1976).
9. Leroy G. Schultz, "The Wife Assaulter," *Corrective Psychiatry and Journal of Social Therapy* 6 (February 1960): 103–11. Schultz illustrates the "blaming-the-victim" approach with this statement (p. 103): "The victims in spouse assaults can always be assumed to have played a crucial role in the offense, and may have directly or indirectly brought about or precipitated their own victimization."

10. Margaret Gates, Introduction to *The Victimization of Women,* eds. Jane Roberts Chapman and Margaret Gates (Beverly Hills, Ca.: SAGE Publications, 1978), 11.
11. R. Emerson Dobash and Russell P. Dobash, "Wives: The 'Appropriate' Victims of Marital Violence," *Victimology: An International Journal* 2, nos. 3–4 (1977–78): 426.
12. Dobash and Dobash, "Wives: The 'Appropriate' Victims of Marital Violence," 429.
13. Terry Davidson, "Wifebeating: A Recurring Phenomenon Throughout History." In *Battered Women: A Psychosociological Study of Domestic Violence,* ed. Maria Roy (New York: Van Nostrand Reinhold, 1977), 14.
14. Davidson, "Wifebeating: A Recurring Phenomenon Throughout History," 18.
15. Elizabeth Pleck, "Wife Beating in Nineteenth-Century America," *Victimology: An International Journal* 4, no. 1 (1979): 61.
16. Cited in Dobash and Dobash, "Wives: The 'Appropriate' Victims of Marital Violence," 431.
17. John Stuart Mill, *The Subjection of Women* (reprint, Cambridge, Mass.: MIT Press, 1970), 30–36.
18. Marvin E. Wolfgang, "Husband-Wife Homicides," *Corrective Psychiatry and Journal of Social Therapy* 2 (1976): 263–71.
19. See Erin Pizzey, *Scream Quietly or the Neighbors Will Hear* (Short Hills, N.J.: Ridley Enslow Publishers, 1977); and Lenore E. Walker, *The Battered Woman* (New York: Harper and Row, 1979).
20. Straus, Gelles, and Steinmetz, *Behind Closed Doors: Violence in the American Family.*
21. See Richard J. Gelles, "No Place to Go: The Social Dynamics of Marital Violence," in *Battered Women,* ed. Maria Roy (New York: Van Nostrand Reinhold, 1977), 418–55.
22. For a concise history of violence toward children, see S. X. Radbill, "A History of Child Abuse and Infanticide," in *The Battered Child,* 2d ed., eds. R. E. Helfer and C. H. Kempe (Chicago: University of Chicago Press, 1974), 3–24; also Jerry J. Sweet and Patricia A. Resick, "The Maltreatment of Children: A Review of Theories and Research," *Journal of Social Issues* 35, no. 2 (1979): 40–59; Lloyd DeMause, "Our Forebearers Made Childhood a Nightmare," *Psychology Today* 8 (April 1975): 85–87.
23. Chase, *A Child Is Being Beaten,* 12–13. For a grislier and more comprehensive history of child abuse, see David Bakan, *Slaughter of the Innocents* (Boston: Beacon Press, 1962).
24. Radbill, "A History of Child Abuse and Infanticide," 3–24.
25. "Executive Summary: National Study of the Incidence and Severity of Child Abuse and Neglect." Report to the National Center on Child Abuse and Neglect, U.S. Department of Health and Human Services (Washington, D.C.: U.S. Government Printing Office, 1982), 3.

26. Lenore E. Walker, *The Battered Woman* (New York: Harper & Row, 1979), xvii.
27. Bonnie Carlson, "Battered Women and Their Assailants," *Social Work* 22 (November 1977): 455–60.

2: WOMEN: THE MOST VISIBLE VICTIMS

1. These two excerpts were taken from sworn testimony at public hearings before the State of Michigan's Women's Commission held September–October, 1976. See Nancy Hammond, ed., *Domestic Assault: A Report of Family Violence in Michigan* (Lansing, Mich.: Michigan Women's Commission, 1977) 28, 48.
2. Lenore E. Walker, *The Battered Woman* (New York: Harper & Row, 1979), 105–6.
3. Elaine Hilberman and Kit Munson, "Sixty Battered Women," *Victimology: An International Journal* 2, nos. 3–4 (1977–78): 462.
4. Walker, *The Battered Woman*, Chapter 7.
5. Hammond, *Domestic Assault: A Report on Family Violence in Michigan*, 34–36.
6. Walker, *The Battered Woman*, 18. Walker concludes: "Most battered women are from middle-class and higher-income homes where the power of their wealth is in the hands of their husbands."
7. George Levinger, "Sources of Marital Dissatisfaction Among Applicants for Divorce," in *Violence in the Family*, eds. Suzanne K. Steinmetz and Murray A. Straus (New York: Harper & Row, 1974), 85; John O'Brien, "Violence in Divorce Prone Families," *Journal of Marriage and the Family* 33 (November 1971): 694; Rodney Stark and James McEvoy III, "Middle Class Violence," *Psychology Today* 4 (November 1970): 52–65.
8. Murray A. Straus, Richard J. Gelles, and Suzanne K. Steinmetz, *Behind Closed Doors: Violence in the American Family* (Garden City, N.Y.: Anchor/Doubleday, 1980). Quotes are from pp. 121, 101, and 109 respectively.
9. Straus, Gelles, and Steinmetz, *Behind Closed Doors*, 122.
10. John P. Flynn, "Recent Findings Related to Wife Abuse," *Social Casework*, 58 (January 1977): 18.
11. Srinika Jayaratne, "Child Abusers as Parents and Children: A Review," *Social Work* 22 (January 1977): 18.
12. Hilberman and Munson, "Sixty Battered Women," 461.
13. Bruce J. Rounsaville, "Theories in Marital Violence: Evidence from a Study of Battered Women," *Victimology: An International Journal* 3, nos. 1–2 (1978).
14. Mildred Daley Pagelow, *Woman Battering: Victims and Their Experiences* (Beverly Hills, Ca.: SAGE Publications, 1981), 145–77.

15. Roger Langley and Richard C. Levy, *Wife Beating: The Silent Crisis* (New York: E. P. Dutton, 1977), 112.
16. Langley and Levy, among others, essentially argue along the same lines in attacking the myth of alcohol/drug use as causing battering. See *Wife Beating: The Silent Crisis*, p. 111.
17. Hilberman and Munson, "Sixty Battered Women," 461–2.
18. This concept is explored in an important article published in the mid-1970s. See Ann W. Burgess and Lynda L. Holmstrom, "Rape Trauma Syndrome," *American Journal of Psychiatry* 131 (1974): 981–86.
19. Walker, *The Battered Woman*, 49–50.
20. Barbara Ann Brown and Gina Rachele Brazzle, "The Self Concept and Marital Satisfaction of Women in Metroplex Shelters," Master's thesis (Arlington, Texas: The University of Texas at Arlington Graduate School of Social Work, 1982), 18.
21. Rounsaville, "Theories in Marital Violence," 16.
22. Brown and Brazzle, "The Self Concept and Marital Satisfaction of Women in Metroplex Shelters," 19.
23. Richard J. Gelles, "No Place to Go: The Social Dynamics of Marital Violence." In *Battered Women*, ed. Maria Roy (New York: Van Nostrand Reinhold, 1977), 60.

3: CHILDREN: THE MOST HELPLESS VICTIMS

1. Keith Anderson, "Speaking for the Victims," *Dallas Morning News*, September 14, 1982.
2. Christine M. deLange (project director), "Summary of Half-Year Progress on Contract #90-CA-880-1." National Center of Child Abuse and Neglect Demonstration and Research Project: *Children from Violent Homes: Intervention and Advocacy.* (Dallas, Texas: Domestic Violence Intervention Alliance of Dallas, Inc., 1982).
3. Val D. MacMurray, "The Effect and Nature of Alcohol Abuse in Cases of Child Neglect," *Victimology: An International Journal* 4, no. 1 (1979): 33.
4. Carroll Brodsky, "Rape at Work," in *Sexual Assault: The Victim and the Rapist*, eds. Marsha J. Walker and Stanley L. Brodsky (Lexington, Mass.: D.C. Heath, 1976), 43.
5. Frank J. Weed, "Child Abuse: American Cultural Values and Parental Relationships," unpublished manuscript (Arlington, Texas: The University of Texas at Arlington, 1981), 2.
6. Ibid., 1.
7. Richard J. Gelles, "Child Abuse as Psychopathology: A Sociological Critique Reformation," *American Journal of Orthopsychiatry* 43 (1973): 611–21.
8. James I. McGovern, "Delicate Inquiry: The Investigator's Role in Child Abuse," *Victimology: An International Journal* 2 (summer 1977): 279–80.

4: MEN: THE PERPETRATORS OF VIOLENCE

1. Lloyd Shearer, "Ingleborg Dedichen: She Was the Great Love of Aristotle Onassis," *Parade* (July 1975): 4–5.
2. Anne Marie Biondo, "Unemployed and Violent: Joblessness and Wife Battering," *Fort Worth Star-Telegram*, September 3, 1982.
3. Ibid.
4. For example, see Geraldine Butts Stahly, "A Review of Select Literature of Spousal Violence," *Victimology: An International Journal* 2, nos. 3–4 (1977–78): 597; and Bruce J. Rounsaville, "Theories in Marital Violence: Evidence From a Study of Battered Women," *Victimology: An International Journal* 3, nos. 1–2 (1978): 19.
5. Leroy J. Schultz, "The Wife Assaulter," *Journal of Social Therapy* 2 (August 1964).
6. Jackson Toby, "Violence and the Masculine Ideal: Some Qualitative Data," in *Violence in the Family*, eds. Suzanne K. Steinmetz and Murray A. Straus (New York: Harper & Row, 1974), 58–65. Our finding that black men are more likely to batter severely than either Hispanic or white men might support this theory if we knew that those black men predominately came from households headed by females. Unfortunately, our information on them is not that detailed.
7. Erin Pizzey, *Scream Quietly or the Neighbors Will Hear* (Short Hills, N.J.: Ridley Enslow Publishers, 1977).
8. Murray Straus, Richard J. Gelles, and Suzanne K. Steinmetz, *Behind Closed Doors: Violence in the American Family* (Garden City, N.Y.: Anchor/Doubleday, 1980).
9. Karen H. Coleman and Paula M. Howard, "Conjugal Violence: What Women Report." Paper presented at the annual meeting of the American Psychological Association, August, 1978, p. 11.
10. Ibid., p. 5.
11. Karen H. Coleman, Mary B. Holley, and Toby Myers, "Sex-Role Stereotypes: They Contribute to Conjugal Violence," unpublished manuscript (Houston: Texas Research Institute of Mental Sciences, 1977), pp. 4–5.

5: AFTER THE BATTERING: A WOMAN'S OPTIONS

1. Del Martin, "Scope of the Problem," in *Battered Women: Issues of Public Policy*. (A Consultation Sponsored by the United States Commission on Civil Rights.) (Washington, D.C.: U.S. Government Printing Office, January 30–31, 1978), p. 223.
2. *Parade*, November 30, 1980.
3. Del Martin, "Scope of the Problem."
4. Robin Stringfellow, "Mrs. Fielder Gets 2-Year Sentence in Spouse's Death," *Dallas Morning News*, October 13, 1982.

6: ANOTHER ALTERNATIVE: SHELTERS FOR BATTERED FAMILIES

1. *Evaluation Report on Family Violence Centers in Texas 1979–1980* (Austin: Children and Family Services, Texas Department of Human Resources, March 1981), 2.
2. Ibid., 2–3.
3. Texas House of Representatives, "An Act relating to shelter and services for victims of family violence and funding for these programs," House Bill No. 1334, 1981.
4. Vivian Castleberry, "Battered Wives—The Volunteer: She Seeks Help From the Community," *Dallas Times Herald,* January 29, 1978.
5. Vivian Castleberry, "Secret Shelter Aids Battered Wives, Children," *Dallas Times Herald,* November 25, 1980.
6. Ibid.
7. *Evaluation Report of Family Violence Centers in Texas 1979–1980,* 7.
8. Karen Mountain, "The Rural Texas Domestic Violence Health Professionals Education Program," unpublished grant proposal (Austin, Texas: 1982), 1.

7: FROM INSULT TO INJURY: THE DEAD ENDS AND POSSIBILITIES OF THE LAW

1. Katie Brown, " 'Domestic Disturbances'—Sensitive Area for Police," *Fort Worth Star-Telegram,* September 2, 1975.
2. See Nancy Loving, *Responding to Spouse Abuse and Wife Beating: A Guide for Police* (Washington, D.C.: Police Executive Research Forum, 1980.
3. Ellen Goodman, "Battered Wives Need Shelters," *Fort Worth Star-Telegram,* September 30, 1980.
4. "DC Wives Unlikely To Report Beatings," *Fort Worth Star-Telegram,* July 11, 1979.
5. " 'Send Wives to Mother,' Senator Says," *Fort Worth Star-Telegram,* April 22, 1981.
6. "Feminists Slap N.H. Rights Panel," *Fort Worth Star-Telegram,* September 15, 1977.
7. *Under the Rule of Thumb: Battered Women and the Administration of Justice: A Report of the United States Commission on Civil Rights* (Washington, D.C.: U.S. Government Printing Office, 1982), 82.
8. Ibid., 84.
9. Brown, " 'Domestic Disturbances'—Sensitive Area for Police."
10. Ibid.
11. *Under The Rule of Thumb,* 33–34.
12. "Battered Wive Told to Burn Mate," *Fort Worth Star-Telegram,* January 11, 1978.

13. See, for example, Representative Barbara Ann Mikulski, quoted in the *Detroit Free Press*, October 11, 1977.
14. Ann Landers, "Assault Charges Bring Unexpected Guilt," *Dallas Morning News*, August 6, 1982.
15. Reprinted by permission of Mary Neal Sisk.
16. Ann Landers, "Time Out Again for Other Women," *Fort Worth Star-Telegram*, October 21, 1982.
17. *Under The Rule of Thumb*, 36.
18. Ibid., 60.
19. Lynne Messina, "Spouse Abuse: Survey Shows Cases Widespread; 80 Percent Unreported," *Austin American-Statesman*, April 19, 1979.
20. Raymond I. Parnas, "The Police Response to the Domestic Disturbance," *Wisconsin Law Review* (Fall 1967): 914.
21. Brown, " 'Domestic Disturbances'—Sensitive Area For Police."
22. John L. Luther, *Family Violence Project: Law Enforcement Survey Component* (Austin: Texas Department of Human Resources, 1980).
23. Brown, " 'Domestic Disturbances'—Sensitive Area For Police."
24. Parnas, "The Police Response to the Domestic Disturbance," 920.
25. Morton Bard, "The Study and Modification of Intra-Familial Violence," in *Violence in the Family*, eds. Suzanne K. Steinmetz and Murray A. Straus (New York: Harper & Row, 1974), 137.
26. Morton Bard, "Family Intervention Police Teams as a Community Mental Health Resource," *The Journal of Criminal Law, Criminology, and Police Science* 6, no. 2 (1969): 248.
27. *Under the Rule of Thumb*, 96.

8: A LOOK AHEAD

1. Mildred Daley Pagelow, *Woman-Battering: Victims and Their Experiences* (Beverly Hills, Ca.: SAGE Publications, 1981), 168–71.
2. Jean Renvoize, *Web of Violence* (London: Routledge & Kegan Paul, 1978), ix.
3. "Police Question Suspect in Torture of Women," *Fort Worth Star-Telegram*, September 26, 1982.
4. See Kim Carlton, "Freeway Assaults: Traffic-related Violence, And Even Homicides, Are Becoming An Every Day Fact," *Houston Chronicle*, February 10, 1982; and Jennifer Bolch, "Hostility On the Highway: If You Get Hit, It Might Be With a Fist Instead of Someone's Car," *Dallas Times Herald*, February 7, 1982.
5. "Schools Growing Stricter on Paddlings," *Fort Worth Star-Telegram*, October 24, 1982.

Select Bibliography on Family Violence

CHILD ABUSE

Arthur, Morton. "Yo-Yo Children: A Study of 23 Violent Matrimonial Cases." In *Battered Women,* edited by Maria Roy, 249–63. New York: Van Nostrand Reinhold, 1977.

Bakan, D. *Slaughter of the Innocents: A Study of the Battered Child Phenomenon.* Boston: Beacon Press, 1971.

Chase, Naomi F. *A Child Is Being Beaten.* New York: McGraw-Hill, 1975.

De Francis, Vincent. "The Status of Child Protective Services: A National Dilemma." In *Helping the Battered Child and His Family,* edited by C. Henry Kempe and Roy E. Helfer, 127–45. Philadelphia: J. P. Lippincott, 1972.

DeMause, Lloyd. "Our Forebearers Made Childhood a Nightmare." *Psychology Today* 8 (April 1975): 85–87.

Elmer, Elizabeth. *Children in Jeopardy.* Pittsburgh: University of Pittsburgh Press, 1967.

Erlanger, Howard S. "Social Class Differences in Parents' Use of Physical Punishment." In *Violence in the Family,* edited by Suzanne K. Steinmetz and Murray A. Straus. New York: Harper & Row, 1974.

Gelles, Richard J. "Demythologizing Child Abuse." *The Family Coordinator* 25 (1976): 135–41.

Gerbner, George; Ross, Catherine J.; and Zigler, Edward, eds. *Child Abuse: An Agenda for Action.* New York: Oxford University Press, 1980.

Gil, David G. "Child Abuse: Levels of Manifestation, Causal Dimensions and Primary Prevention." *Victimology: An International Journal* 2, no. 2 (1977): 186–94.

Gil, David G. "A Conceptual Model of Child Abuse and Its Implications for Social Policy." In *Violence in the Family,* edited by Suzanne K. Steinmetz and Murray A. Straus. New York: Harper & Row, 1974.

Gil, David G. *Violence Against Children.* Cambridge, Massachusetts: Harvard University Press, 1970.

Green, Arthur H. "Societal Neglect of Child Abusing Parents." *Victimology: An International Journal* 2, no. 2 (1977): 285–93.

Jayaratne, Srinika. "Child Abusers as Parents and Children: A Review." *Social Work* 22 (January 1977): 5–9.

Libbey, Patricia and Bybee, Roger. "The Physical Abuse of Adolescents." *Journal of Social Issues* 35, no. 2 (1979): 101–26.

Lourie, Ira S. "The Phenomenon of the Abused Adolescent: A Clinical Study." *Victimology: An International Journal* 2, no. 2 (1977): 268–76.

MacMurray, Val D. "The Effect and Nature of Alcohol Abuse in Cases of Child Neglect." *Victimology: An International Journal* 4, no. 1 (1979): 29–45.

Maden, Marc F. and Wrench, David G. "Significant Findings in Child Abuse Research." *Victimology: An International Journal* 2, no. 2 (1977): 196–224.

Martin, H. P.; Beezley, P.; Conway, E. F.; and Kempe, C. H. "The Development of Abused Children: A Review of the Literature and Physical, Neurologic, and Intellectual Findings." *Advances in Pediatrics* 21 (1974): 25–73.

Radbill, S. X. "A History of Child Abuse and Infanticide." In *The Battered Child*. 2d ed., edited by R. E. Helfer and C. H. Kempe, 3–24. Chicago: University of Chicago Press, 1974.

Sweet, Jerry J. and Resick, Patricia A. "The Maltreatment of Children. A Review of Theories and Research." *Journal of Social Issues* 35, no. 2 (1979): 40–59.

WOMAN ABUSE

Bach, George R. and Wyden, Peter. "Why Intimates Must Fight." In *Violence in the Family*, edited by Suzanne K. Steinmetz and Murray A. Straus, 98–110. New York: Harper & Row, 1974.

Ball, Patricia G. and Wyman, Elizabeth. "Battered Wives and Powerlessness: What Can Counselors Do?" *Victimology: An International Journal* 2, nos. 3–4 (1977–78): 545–52.

Boudouris, J. "Homicide and the Family." *Journal of Marriage and the Family* 33 (November 1971): 667–73.

Brown, Barbara Ann and Brazzle, Gina Rachele. "The Self Concept and Marital Satisfaction of Women in Metroplex Shelters." Master's thesis, University of Texas, Arlington, 1982.

Brown, M. M.; Aguire, B. E.; and Jorgensen, Carol. "Abusers of Clients of Women's Shelters: Their Socialization and Resources." *Journal of Sociology and Social Welfare* 8 (September 1981): 462–70.

Burgess, Ann W. and Holmstrom, Lynda L. "Rape Trauma Syndrome." *American Journal of Psychiatry* 131 (1974): 981–86.

Carlson, Bonnie E. "Battered Women and Their Assailants." *Social Work* 22 (November 1977): 455–60.

Dobash, R. Emerson and Dobash, Russell P. "Wives: The 'Appropriate' Victims of Marital Violence." *Victimology: An International Journal* 2, nos. 3–4 (1977–78): 426–42.

Dobash, R. Emerson and Dobash, Russell P. "Wife-Beating—Still a Common Form of Violence." *Social Work Today* 9 (1977): 14–17.

Flemming, Jennifer Baker. *Stopping Wife Abuse.* Garden City, New York: Anchor Press/Doubleday, 1979.

Gelles, Richard J. "Abused Wives: Why Do They Stay?" *Journal of Marriage and the Family* 38 (November 1976): 659–68.

Hammond, Nancy, ed. *Domestic Assault: A Report on Family Violence in Michigan.* Lansing, Michigan: Michigan Women's Commission, 1977.

Hanks, S. E. and Rosenbaum, C. P. "Battered Women: A Study of Women Who Live with Violent Alcohol-Abusing Men." *American Journal of Orthopsychiatry* 47, no. 2 (1977): 291–306.

Hilberman, E. "Overview: The 'Wife-beater's Wife' Reconsidered." *American Journal of Psychiatry* 137 (1980): 1336–47.

Hilberman, Elaine and Munson, Kit. "Sixty Battered Women." *Victimology: An International Journal* 2, nos. 3-4 (1978): 460–70.

Langley, Roger and Levy, Richard C. *Wife Beating: The Silent Crisis.* New York: E. P. Dutton, 1977.

Martin, Del. *Battered Wives.* San Francisco: Glide Publications, 1976.

McNulty, Faith. *The Burning Bed.* New York: Harcourt Brace Jovanovich, 1980.

Moore, Donna M. *Battered Women.* Beverly Hills: SAGE Publications, 1979.

Pleck, Elizabeth. "Wife Beating in Nineteenth Century America." *Victimology: An International Journal* 4, no. 1 (1979): 60–74.

Petro, J. A.; Quann, P. L.; and Graham, W. P. III. "Wife Abuse: The Diagnosis and Its Implications." *Journal of the American Medical Association* 240 (1978): 240–41.

Pizzey, Erin. *Scream Quietly or the Neighbors Will Hear.* Short Hills, N.J.: Ridley Enslow Publishers, 1977.

Rounsaville, Bruce J. "Theories in Marital Violence: Evidence from a Study of Battered Women." *Victimology: An International Journal* 3, nos. 1–2 (1978): 11–31.

Roy, Maria, ed. *Battered Women: A Psychological Study of Domestic Violence.* New York: Van Nostrand Reinhold, 1977.

Schultz, Leroy G. "The Wife Assaulter." *Corrective Psychiatry and Journal of Social Therapy* 6 (February 1960): 103–11.

Snell, John E.; Rosenwald, Richard J.; and Robey, Ames. "The Wifebeater's Wife: A Study of Family Interaction." *Archives of General Psychiatry* 11 (August 1964): 107–13.

Straus, Murray A. "Wife Beating: How Common and Why?" *Victimology: An International Journal* 2, nos. 3–4 (1977–78): 443–58.

Truninger, Elizabeth. "Marital Violence: The Legal Solutions." *The Hastings Law Journal* 23 (November 1971): 259–76.

Waites, Elizabeth A. "Female Masochism and the Enforced Restriction of Choice." *Victimology: An International Journal* 2, nos. 3-4 (1977–78): 535–44.

Walker, Lenore E. *The Battered Woman*. New York: Harper & Row, 1979.

Walker, Lenore E. "Battered Women and Learned Helplessness." *Victimology: An International Journal* 2, nos. 3–4 (1977–78): 525–34.

GENERAL FAMILY VIOLENCE

Baher, Edwina, et al. *At Risk*. Boston: Routledge & Kegan Paul, 1976.

Bard, Morton. "The Study and Modification of Intra-Family Violence." In *Violence in the Family*, edited by Suzanne K. Steinmetz and Murray A. Straus, 127–39. New York: Harper & Row, 1974.

Bard, Morton. "Family Intervention Police Teams as a Community Mental Health Resource." *The Journal of Criminal Law, Criminology, and Police Science* 60 (June 1969): 247–50.

Bard, Morton. "Family Crisis Intervention: From Concept to Implementation." In *Battered Women*, edited by Maria Roy, 172–92. New York: Van Nostrand Reinhold, 1977.

Bard, Morton. *The Function of Police in Crisis Intervention and Conflict Management*. Washington, D.C.: U.S. Department of Justice, Law Enforcement Assistance Administration, 1975: 6.9–6.10.

Bard, Morton and Zacher, Joseph. "The Prevention of Family Violence: Dilemmas of Community Intervention." *Journal of Marriage and the Family* 33 (November 1971): 677–82.

Berland, Marie, ed. *Violence in the Family*. Manchester: Manchester University Press, 1976.

Gelles, Richard J. "No Place to Go: The Social Dynamics of Marital Violence." In *Battered Women*, edited by Maria Roy, 46–63. New York: Van Nostrand Reinhold, 1977.

Gelles, Richard J. *The Violent Home*. Beverly Hills: SAGE Publications, 1974.

Gelles, Richard J. and Straus, Murray A. "Violence in the American Family." *Journal of Social Issues* 35, no. 2 (1979): 15–39.

Goode, William J. "Force and Violence in the Family." *Journal of Marriage and the Family* 33 (November 1971): 624–36.

Levinger, George. "Sources of Marital Dissatisfaction Among Applicants for Divorce." *American Journal of Orthopsychiatry* 36 (October 1966): 803–7.

O'Brien, John E. "Violence in Divorce Prone Families." *Journal of Marriage and the Family* 33 (November 1971): 692–98.

Parnas, Raymond I. "The Police Response to the Domestic Disturbance." *Wisconsin Law Review* (Fall 1967): 914–60.

Renvoize, Jean. *Web of Violence*. Boston: Routledge & Kegan Paul, 1978.

Scanzoni, John. *Sexual Bargaining.* Englewood Cliffs, N.J.: Prentice-Hall, 1972.

Stark, Rodney and McEvoy, James III. "Middle Class Violence." *Psychology Today* 4 (November 1970): 52–65.

Steinmetz, Suzanne K. "The Use of Force for Resolving Family Conflict: The Training Ground for Abuse." *The Family Coordinator* 26 (January 1977): 19–26.

Steinmetz, Suzanne K. "The Battered Husband Syndrome." *Victimology: An International Journal* 2, nos. 3–4 (1977–78): 499–509.

Steinmetz, Suzanne K. *The Cycle of Violence: Assertive, Aggressive, and Abusive Family Interaction.* New York: Praeger, 1977.

Steinmetz, Suzanne K. and Straus, Murray, eds. *Violence in the Family.* New York: Dodd, Mead & Company, 1974.

Straus, Murray A. "A General Systems Theory Approach to the Development of a Theory of Violence Between Family Members." *Social Science Information* 22 (June 1973): 105–25.

Straus, Murray; Gelles, Richard J.; and Steinmetz, Suzanne K. *Behind Closed Doors: Violence in the American Family.* Garden City, New York: Anchor Press/Doubleday, 1980.

Index

William A. Stacey and Anson Shupe are sociologists at the University of Texas at Arlington and coauthors of a book on the New Right, *Born-Again Politics and the Moral Majority.* For their work on domestic violence they received an award from the Texas Council on Family Violence.

Anson Shupe has also done extensive research on religious cults and is coauthor with David Bromley of *Strange Gods* (Beacon Press).